Hiking Waterfalls in Georgia and South Carolina

A Guide to the States' Best Waterfall Hikes

Melissa Watson

FALCONGUIDES

GUILFORD, CONNECTICUT
HELENA, MONTANA

AN IMPRINT OF **ROWMAN & LITTLEFIELD**

For Mom:
You are my best friend, my mentor, and my inspiration.
Your editorial excellence shines through these pages.
Thank you for being you!

FALCONGUIDES®

Copyright © 2011 by Rowman & Littlefield

ALL RIGHTS RESERVED. No part of this book may be reproduced or transmitted in any form by any means, electronic or mechanical, including photocopying and recording, or by any information storage and retrieval system, except as may be expressly permitted in writing from the publisher.

FalconGuides is an imprint of Rowman & Littlefield.

Falcon, FalconGuides, and Outfit Your Mind are registered trademarks of Rowman & Littlefield

Maps: Trailhead Graphics Inc. © Rowman & Littlefield
TOPO! Explorer software and SuperQuad source maps courtesy of National Geographic Maps. For information about TOPO! Explorer, TOPO!, and Nat Geo Maps products, go to www.topo.com or www.natgeo maps.com.
Photos: Melissa Watson

Distributed by NATIONAL BOOK NETWORK

Library of Congress Cataloging-in-Publication Data

Watson, Melissa.
  Hiking waterfalls in Georgia and South Carolina : a guide to the states' best waterfall hikes / Melissa Watson.
     p. cm.
  ISBN 978-0-7627-7151-6
  1. Hiking–Georgia–Guidebooks. 2. Hiking–South Carolina–Guidebooks. 3. Waterfalls–Georgia–Guidebooks. 4. Waterfalls–South Carolina–Guidebooks. 5. Georgia–Guidebooks. 6. South Carolina–Guidebooks. I. Title.
  GV199.42.G46W38 2011
  917.5–dc23

                              2011026400

Printed in the United States of America

Contents

Georgia Waterfalls

Overview

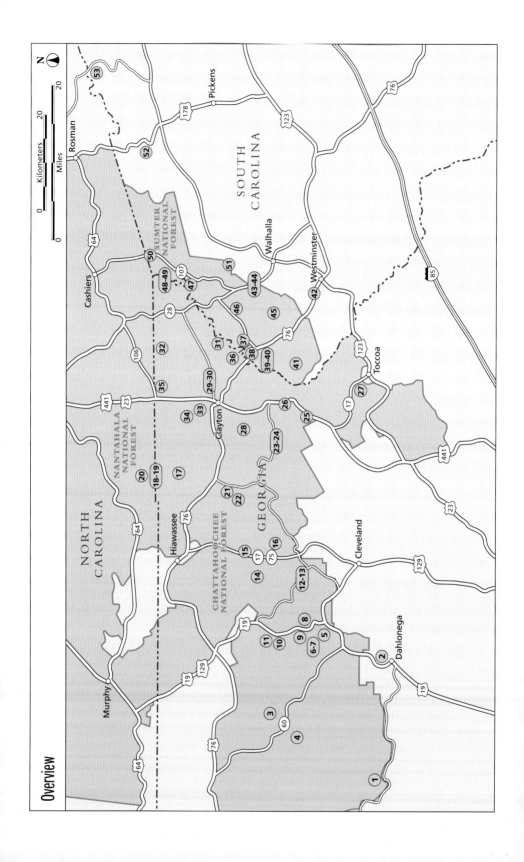

South Carolina Waterfalls

Acknowledgments

I'd like to thank my family for their love, patience, and support: Terri Sansonetti; Maria, Frazier, Christina, and Cory Payton; Doug Watson; Sue, Tom, Frank, Amy, Thomas, Joe, Kristen, Rebecca, Nathaniel, Katilee, Mark, Jonathon, and Joshua Strazza; Michelle, Roland, and Lucas Arisolo; Maris Herold; and Rachel Saunders. I love you all!

Many people were helpful in confirming the accuracy of the hikes contained within. I'd like the following people to know how thankful I am for their investment of time and their wealth of knowledge: Curtis Phillabaum and Melissa Dolinsky at the Palm Beach Zoo, David Reams at the Chattooga Ranger District of the Chattahoochee National Forest, Traci Bash at Caesars Head State Park, Mountain Bridge Wilderness Area, Anthony Lampros and Tracy English at Black Rock Mountain State Park, Bill Tanner at Amicalola State Park, Randy Gambrell at Vogel State Park, and Toni King at Tallulah Gorge State Park.

Finally I'd like to thank the following people for covering my shifts at the firehouse so that I could spend six weeks in the woods, rehiking every trail in this book: Jeff McCord, George Donechie, Donny Brown, Joe Bostic, Travis Thomas, and of course, my crew at Station 51—Craig Hatton, Chris Uzzo, Jody Miedema, Jason Alexander, and Mike Osuna—for their patience and tolerance while I diligently worked on this project.

Introduction

Waterfalls are magical, mysterious wonders of nature. From small cascades to tall, free-falling water, each has a character and beauty of its own.

I have been entranced by the magic of waterfalls my entire life, and now, after spending the past twenty years seeking out new falls and revisiting old favorites, I'm sharing that passion. For months at a time I have hiked and camped and reveled in the waterfalls of Georia and South Carolina. Some of this time was spent in frustration, though, due to inaccurate trail or driving directions. And so I began writing this book with one goal in mind—accuracy. Setting out with my dog Mikey in tow, I hiked and rehiked each trail in this book while documenting the details along the way. I ended up hiking hundreds of miles and driving thousands of miles so that you wouldn't have to.

Once I gathered my field notes together, I began the laborious task of putting them into writing. I've provided specific trail directions and thorough driving directions. I've also included GPS coordinates and the appropriate *DeLorme: Atlas & Gazetteer* map page and coordinates to assist you on your quest to find the falls.

While I was finishing up some of the more entertaining text of this guidebook, I discovered the strangest thing—my muse, which happened to come in the form of champagne and show tunes. I found my fingers tip tapping away on the keyboard to the likes of *The Phantom of the Opera* and *The Sound of Music*. I can't tell you how many times I heard Julie Andrews sing "Do-Re-Mi" as the words flowed onto my computer screen. Pandora radio really is fabulous but repetitive, and I can now say with a smile, that I know every word to *The Jungle Book's* "The Bare Necessities" song.

I hope you find this book entertaining as well as accurate. Within these pages you will find mention and description of eighty-two waterfalls for your viewing pleasure—from roadside beauties to those set deep in the forest. Enjoy this user-friendly guide as it leads you to the most magnificent waterfalls in Georgia and South Carolina, plus a couple just over the border in North Carolina. Don your hiking boots and grab your camera—a world of discovery lies ahead.

How to Use This Guide

The waterfalls in this guide have been divided into geographic areas. This way, when you plan to visit a certain town, you can easily see which waterfalls are nearby. A detailed map of the trails and their surroundings is provided for each area.

Along with each map you'll find the hikes shown on that map. Each hike in this guide is presented in the same format, which begins with a brief description of the waterfall, from the author's perspective.

Next come the hike "specs": important information starting off with waterfall height and my personal beauty rating for each waterfall. Next is the trail distance (always the out and back, total distance for the recommended hike). But sometimes it's not a hike. Sometimes you can see the waterfall from the roadside or parking

Discover Georgia's Anna Ruby Falls, where York Creek flows to meet Smith Creek (hike 16).

area. Then you'll find difficulty (how much exertion the trail will require), trail surface, and blaze color; approximate hiking time; and other trail users you might encounter. I have also noted the county in which the waterfall is located, land status (national forest/park, private owner, etc.), trail contacts, and FYI (for your information) for additional information on the area and any other important information, such as park hours and whether a fee is charged.

Lastly you will find the relevant *DeLorme: Georgia Atlas & Gazetteer* (2010, 6th edition), *DeLorme: South Carolina Atlas & Gazetteer* (2006, 3rd edition), and *DeLorme: North Carolina Atlas & Gazetteer* (2010, 9th edition) page and coordinates to supplement the maps provided in this guide. I highly recommend getting the *DeLorme Atlas & Gazetteer* for any state in which you plan to hike. They've been of great help to me on my explorations. The National Geographic Trails Illustrated topographic maps are another useful tool and an invaluable resource when navigating through the mountains of the Chattahoochee, Sumter, and Nantahala National Forests.

Following the hike specs you will see "Finding the trailhead." Because you can't enjoy the hike if you can't find the trailhead, I have provided explicit driving directions, usually from two points of reference, using either a main intersection or a state line as your starting point.

Many of the trailheads are located on USDA Forest Service roads. Most of them are unmarked dirt roads, and there may be several of these in a given area. For this reason, I have given specific driving distances in mileage rounded to the nearest 0.1 mile. I've also tried to give you the best route to the trailhead. So if you see what appears to be a shortcut on the map, chances are there's a good reason I didn't send you that way. (**Note:** When parking near a forest service gate, be sure not to block the gate, and try to leave room for others when parking in pull-offs.)

While I prefer a good old-fashioned map and compass, more and more people are becoming adept at using the Global Positioning System. I therefore have provided GPS coordinates for both the trailheads and waterfalls.

"The Hike" is where you'll find a general description of what to expect along the trail. I've also included a brief history for each waterfall, perhaps how the falls got its name or some interesting information about the area. I personally learned quite a bit while researching this portion of the book and found some of the folklore to be thoroughly entertaining. I hope you do as well.

The "Miles and Directions" provide thorough hiking directions. Any questionable turn, every fork, and every T junction have been documented. I've given you the distance at which you will reach them and also provided left/right directions with corresponding compass direction.

I've worked very hard to keep you from getting lost, but please remember that trails do change over time, as do the waterfalls. The appearance of a waterfall may change with each rainfall, or lack thereof, and with every season. This is the reason I

Middle Brasstown Falls, aka Brasstown Veil, is one of South Carolina's finest (hike 41).

return to the same waterfalls time and time again, and yet I'm always greeted with a new experience.

For Your Safety

Before you hit the trails, there's some important information you should know to help keep you safe and sound.

Know your limits. If I say that a trail or portion of trail is for experienced hikers only, I mean it. This means no children either. Some of the trails presented in this book are extremely steep and potentially dangerous. Please heed my warnings and hike within your limits.

Carry the essentials. Next are the "10 Essential Items" every hiker should carry: map, compass, flashlight, first-aid kit, knife, waterproof matches, candle or fire starter, extra clothing, food, and lots of water. Better to have these things and not need them than to need them and not have them. You will find every one of these items (plus some others) in my day pack at all times.

Give someone your itinerary. Whether you hike in a group or especially if you hike by yourself, always tell people where you'll be hiking and when you expect to

Weather changes quickly in the mountains, so be sure to dress in layers.

return. If there's a place to sign in at the trailhead, please do so prior to hiking. And don't forget to sign out when you return.

Watch for the blazes. For those of you new to hiking, blazes are colored markers on a tree or other natural surface that indicate where the trail goes. Not all trails have blazes, but for those that do I have listed the blaze color in the hike specs. Be aware that the blazes on some trails may be few and far between. And two blazes together on the same surface indicate that there is a sharp turn in the trail ahead.

Dress in layers, and always bring rain gear; it can protect you from rain, wind, and cold. Weather conditions can change rapidly and drastically in the mountains, so try to get a weather report prior to hiking. It pays to be prepared.

Wear the right footwear. It's extremely easy to twist an ankle or stub a toe while hiking. Hiking boots are a simple way to prevent this. Wear good hiking boots or trail runners, and break them in prior to hiking—you don't want to ruin your hike with blisters.

Carry a towel in your pack. Some trails call for fording creeks, and you don't want to hike with cold, wet feet. Not to mention that you may want to take a dip. I swear by chamois-style pack towels, available at local outfitters or REI. They're lightweight, compact, and dry very quickly.

Know where you've been. Here's a helpful hint when hiking on unfamiliar trails: Make it a habit to turn around and look at the trail from the other direction after taking a fork or T. This way, when you're hiking back out, it will look familiar and you won't miss any crucial turns.

Be careful at the brink. Do not play at, around, or near the brink of any waterfall! I cannot stress this enough. Every year people die at waterfalls, and I guarantee they never thought it would happen to them.

Do not climb the face of any waterfall. Countless injuries, even deaths, have been attributed to this as well. Always remember that the rocks and terrain around any waterfall are dangerously slippery, regardless of how surefooted you may be.

Respect the water. Lastly, be aware of how strong the currents can be at both the brink and the base of waterfalls. Never cross at the brink of a waterfall; and if you choose to take a dip at the base, look before you leap. Rocks and trees might lie beneath the surface, and currents may be strong. Choose your swimming holes wisely.

Taking Care of Mother Nature

Many creatures make their home in the forest. As you hike, remember that you are a guest on their terrain; respect them and the forest that harbors them. Try to live by the philosophy of "Take nothing but pictures; leave nothing but footprints." Every stone in the creek, every wildflower along the trail, has its purpose within the ecosystem. Please do not remove these or any items, except litter, from the forest.

A camera is an added bonus to your pack. When you see wildflowers in bloom, you can take their beauty home with you on film or memory card while leaving them for others to appreciate as well.

To get this privileged view of Oceana Falls, you need a permit to hike Georgia's Tallulah Gorge (hike 26).

Note: Federal law prohibits picking wildflowers; removing stones, feathers, or any other natural artifacts; and harassing wildlife in national parks. And it's a pretty good idea for other jurisdictions as well—leave nature as you found it.

Practice "pack it in, pack it out" hiking. If you bring food into the woods, also bring a trash bag to carry out the wrappers and remnants, including orange peels. There's nothing worse than arriving at the base of a stunning waterfall and finding it littered with human debris. I especially ask that you not litter the trails I have shared with you.

Last but not least, please do not shortcut the trails. If you see a shortcut between switchbacks, I implore you to resist the temptation to take it. Stay on the main trail. Shortcutting not only destroys valuable vegetation and creates erosion but also makes the trails much harder to follow.

Happy trails!

Trail Finder

Author's Favorite Waterfalls

10   Helton Creek Falls
12   Raven Cliffs Falls (Georgia)
15   High Shoals Falls
21   Hemlock Falls
25   Panther Creek Falls
26   Waterfalls of Tallulah Gorge
27   Toccoa Falls
30   Martin Creek Falls
39   Opossum Creek Falls
40   Long Creek Falls
41   Brasstown Falls
43   Yellow Branch Falls
52   Twin Falls

Best Swimming Holes

5   Falls #1 on Waters Creek
6   Falls #2 on Waters Creek
10   Helton Creek Falls (Upper)
15   High Shoals Falls (Blue Hole)
22   Sliding Rock on Wildcat Creek
25   Panther Creek Falls
26   Tallulah Gorge (Bridal Veil Falls)
28   Stonewall Falls

Most Crowded Waterfalls

1   Amicalola Falls
9   DeSoto Falls
10   Helton Creek Falls
12   Raven Cliffs Falls (Georgia)
13   Dukes Creek Falls
14   Horse Trough Falls
16   Anna Ruby Falls
24   Minnehaha Falls
25   Panther Creek Falls
26   Waterfalls of Tallulah Gorge
27   Toccoa Falls

33   Ada-Hi Falls
42   Chau Ram Falls
44   Issaqueena Falls
52   Twin Falls
53   Raven Cliff Falls (South Carolina)

Least Crowded Waterfalls

4   Little Rock Creek Falls
7   Crow Mountain Creek Falls
8   Little Ridge Creek Falls
17   Flat Branch Falls
18   Denton Branch Falls
19   Bull Cove Falls (North Carolina)
20   Falls on Deep Gap Branch (North Carolina)
31   Dicks Creek Falls
38   Falls on Reedy Branch

Roadside Waterfalls

6   Falls #2 on Waters Creek
11   Trahlyta Falls
22   Sliding Rock on Wildcat Creek
28   Stonewall Falls
34   Sylvan Mill Falls
35   Eastatoah Falls
42   Chau Ram Falls

Best Waterfall Hikes for Backcountry Camping

12   Raven Cliffs Falls (Georgia)
20   Falls on Deep Gap Branch (North Carolina)
25   Panther Creek Falls
30   Martin Creek Falls
39   Opossum Creek Falls

Map Legend

Transportation

- 85   Interstate Highway
- 76   U.S. Highway
- 28   State Highway
- 2658   Forest/Local Road

Trails

- -------   Featured Trail
- - - - - -   Trail

Water Features

- Body of Water
- River/Creek
- Springs
- Waterfall

Land Management

- - - - - -   State Line
- National Forest
- State Park

Symbols

- Bridge
- ▲ Campground
- — Dam
- Lodge
- ▲ Mountain Peak/Summit
- P Parking
- Pass/Gap
- Picnic Area
- ■ Point of Interest/Structure
- ○ Town
- ① Trailhead
- Viewpoint/Overlook
- ? Visitor/Information Center

Georgia Waterfalls

A pristine pool awaits at Blue Hole Falls (hike 15).

1 Amicalola Falls

Majestic! This impressive waterfall has the claim to fame of being Georgia's tallest, falling 729 feet as it makes its way down the mountainside. Amicalola Falls is so tall that it is difficult to see it all at once. Each section you can view, however, is well worth the visit. The falls can be reached by climbing the many man-made steps or via an alternative route, which is accessible for those in wheelchairs or with strollers.

Height: 729 feet
Beauty rating: Excellent
Distance: hiking trail, 0.6 mile out and back (wheelchair-accessible route, 0.5 mile)
Difficulty: Moderate to strenuous (easy to moderate for wheelchair-accessible route)
Trail surface: Paved path and man-made steps; crushed recycled tire material
Approximate hiking time: 30 minutes
Blaze color: No blazes

County: Dawson
Land status: State park
Trail contact: Amicalola Falls State Park; (706) 265-4703; www.gastateparks.org/ AmicalolaFalls
FYI: Open daily 7 a.m. to 10 p.m.; day-use fee is required to visit the falls.
Maps: DeLorme: Georgia Atlas & Gazetteer: Page 14 G4

Finding the trailhead: From the junction of GA 52 and GA 9, drive west on GA 52 for 13.8 miles. Turn right onto Amicalola Falls State Park Road at the sign for AMICALOLA FALLS STATE PARK AND LODGE and travel for 0.7 mile to where the road dead-ends.

From the junction of GA 52 and GA 183, drive east on GA 52 for 1.45 miles. Turn left onto Amicalola Falls State Park Road at the sign for AMICALOLA FALLS STATE PARK AND LODGE and follow the directions above.

The trailhead is located at the northwest end of the parking lot at the trail information sign-post. GPS: N34 33.805/W84 14.814

To access the ADA parking area for the alternative hiking route: Once inside the park, turn left onto Top of the Falls Road and travel for 0.9 mile to a right turn into the ADA parking area. GPS: N34 33.921/W84 14.931

The Hike

From the trailhead, hike around the pond; the stone path quickly leads to a foot-bridge. Cross the bridge and the paved path begins a steep ascent that you'll follow for the remainder of the way to the lower observation deck of Amicalola Falls.

The trail continues to climb as you make your way up the 175 steps of the man-made stairway to reach a bridge over the falls at the upper observation deck. This vantage point offers the best close-up and personal view of Amicalola Falls.

The trail then continues across the falls and up another 425 steps to the brink of the falls. (**Note:** You can also reach the brink of the falls by driving up Top of the Falls Road and parking at the lot signed for UPPER AMPHITHEATER. You cannot see

Only a small portion of Amicalola Falls' 729-foot drop can be seen at a time.

the waterfall from the brink, but the creek runs through a lovely picnic area, and the views of the surrounding mountainsides are spectacular.)

Alternative route: From the ADA parking area, hike in a generally easterly direction for approximately 0.25 mile until you arrive at the bridge over the falls at the upper observation deck for Amicalola Falls. Although this trail is wheelchair accessible, there is a bit of a grade to it.

Cherokee for "tumbling waters," Amicalola does just that. It is not only the tallest waterfall in Georgia but also the tallest cascading waterfall east of the Mississippi River.

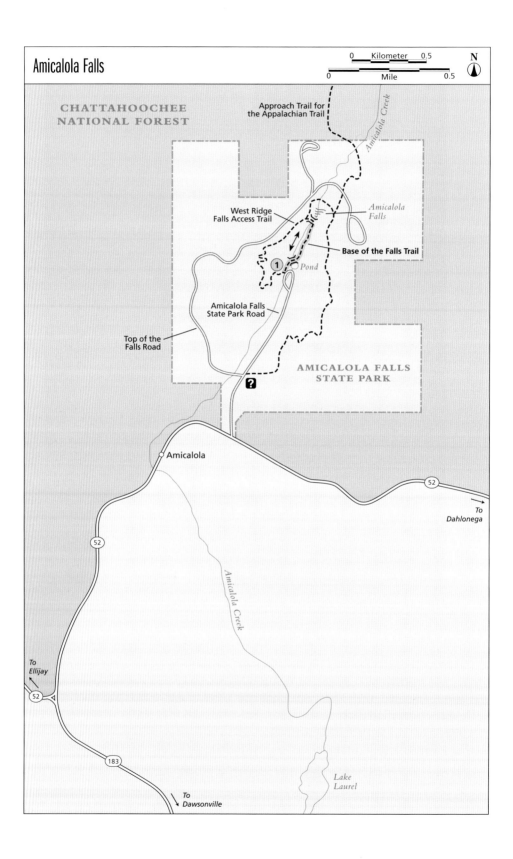

Amicalola Falls

CHATTAHOOCHEE
NATIONAL FOREST

Amicalola Creek

Approach Trail for
the Appalachian Trail

Amicalola
Falls

West Ridge
Falls Access Trail

Base of the Falls Trail

1 Pond

Amicalola Falls
State Park Road

Top of the
Falls Road

AMICALOLA FALLS
STATE PARK

Amicalola

52

To
Dahlonega

52

Amicalola Creek

To
Ellijay

52

183

Lake
Laurel

To
Dawsonville

A trail tree points the way.

The park, which has a long-term parking area, was designed and created to give "thru-hikers" of the Appalachian Trail (AT) a good starting point. The Southern Terminus Approach Trail for the AT takes you up the Amicalola Falls Trail, passes the falls, and then continues to Springer Mountain, where the AT begins (or ends, depending on the direction you hike it).

Miles and Directions

0.0 Start by going around the pond to the left and hiking north-northeast back into the woods. The trail quickly leads to a footbridge. Cross the bridge and continue hiking northeast on the paved path as it makes a steep ascent.

0.2 Arrive at the lower observation deck for the falls. (N34 33.978/W84 14.715). From here the trail leads up a staircase of 175 steps.

0.3 Arrive at the upper observation deck for Amicalola Falls (N34 34.011/W84 14.686). Return the way you came.

0.6 Arrive back at the trailhead.

2 Cane Creek Falls

Uplifting! The true and steady waters of Cane Creek Falls flow with certainty, uplifting and inspiring the viewer. Cane Creek Falls is located on private property within Camp Glisson. The property owners have been kind enough to share this natural wonder with the public, so please be sure to follow all the rules and regulations during your visit. Check in at the gate or Welcome Center prior to visiting the falls, and remember: If you pack it in, pack it out!

Height: 40 feet
Beauty rating: Excellent
Distance: 0.4 mile out and back
Difficulty: Easy
Trail surface: Paved road
Approximate hiking time: 20 minutes
Blaze color: No blazes

County: Lumpkin
Land status: Private property
Trail contact: Camp Glisson; (706) 864-6181; www.campglisson.org
FYI: Camp Glisson is open 8 a.m. to 5 p.m.
Maps: *DeLorme: Georgia Atlas & Gazetteer:* Page 15 G7

Finding the trailhead: From the junction of GA 60 Business and US 19, drive south on GA 60 Business for 2.1 miles. Turn right turn onto Camp Glisson Road and travel for 0.6 mile to a fork in the road. Bear left at the fork and enter Camp Glisson. Drive up the hill and turn right onto Waightsail Henry Way. Immediately pull into the parking lot on your left and park at the Welcome Center.

From the junction of GA 60 Business and GA 52, drive north on GA 60 Business for 2.6 miles. Turn left turn onto Camp Glisson Road and follow the directions above.

GPS: N34 33.454 / W84 00.444

The Hike

The trail follows the paved Camp Glisson Road from the welcome center, around the gate, and farther into the private property of Camp Glisson. After hiking a short downhill, the trail veers off to the right and leads to an observation deck alongside the creek at the brink of the falls. From here, follow the decking back out onto the paved road.

Continue to follow the road farther into Camp Glisson and you soon come to Fred Glisson Circle on your right. Go right here, following Fred Glisson Circle steeply downhill. At the bottom of the hill a footpath on your right leads north a very short distance to the base of Cane Creek Falls.

Camp Glisson was founded by the Reverend Fred Glisson, who held the first youth camp here in the summer of 1925. Camp sessions are still held here, and public access is prohibited when camp is in session. For more information, use the contact information provided above.

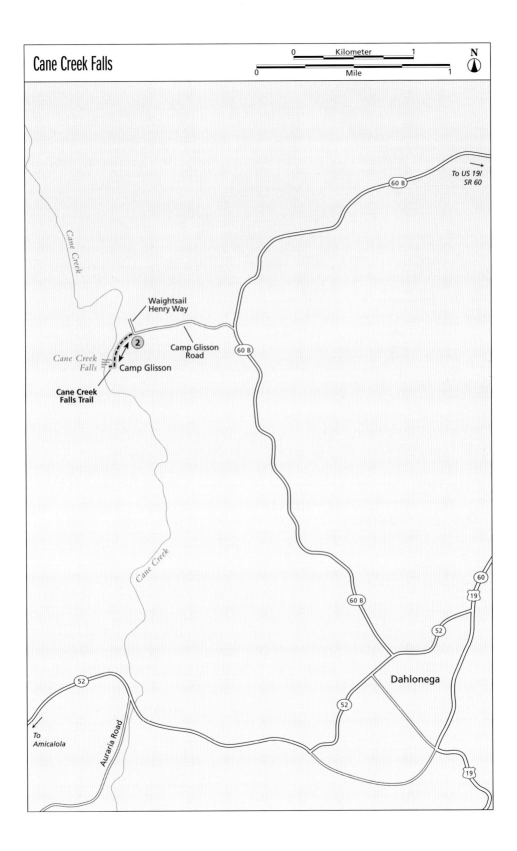

Cane Creek Falls

0   Kilometer   1

0   Mile   1

N

To US 19/
SR 60

60 B

Cane Creek

Waightsail
Henry Way

Camp Glisson
Road

60 B

Cane Creek
Falls

2

Camp Glisson

**Cane Creek
Falls Trail**

Cane Creek

60 B

60

19

52

Dahlonega

52

52

52

To
Amicalola

Auraria Road

19

Cane Creek Falls is a gift from God.

Miles and Directions

0.0 From the parking area, hike southwest past the gate and down the paved road.

0.1 A side road forks off to the right and leads to an observation deck at the brink of the falls. Follow the decking back to the paved road. Head right and continue hiking southwest as you make your way farther into Camp Glisson.

0.2 Come to a paved road on right named Fred Glisson Circle. Go right here (west-northwest) and follow Fred Glisson Circle steeply downhill. A path at the bottom of the hill leads north a short distance to the base of Cane Creek Falls (N34 33.328 / W84 00.547). Return the way you came.

0.4 Arrive back at the trailhead.

3 Sea Creek Falls

Seclusion! If it's seclusion you're seeking, this is the waterfall for you. Although it is a short and easy hike, this one doesn't get much traffic. Why, I have no idea, because the way Sea Creek Falls flows perfectly into its own hidden cove is exceptional.

Height: 25 feet
Beauty rating: Excellent
Distance: 0.4 mile out and back
Difficulty: Easy
Trail surface: Hard-packed dirt
Approximate hiking time: 20 minutes
Blaze color: No blazes

County: Fannin
Land status: National forest
Trail contact: Chattahoochee National Forest, Blue Ridge Ranger District; (706) 745-6928; www.fs.fed.us
Maps: *DeLorme: Georgia Atlas & Gazetteer:* Page 15 D6

Finding the trailhead: From the junction of GA 60 and GA 180, drive north on GA 60 for 10.7 miles. Turn right onto Cooper Creek Road at the sign for Cooper Creek Recreation Area. (***Note:*** You will pass one Cooper Creek Road on your way north on GA 60. *Do not* take this route. Continue until you've gone the full 10.7 miles and arrived at the *second* Cooper Creek Road.) After turning onto Cooper Creek Road, travel 2.9 miles and turn left onto FS 264 at the sign for Sea Creek (along the way, Cooper Creek Road becomes FS 4). Turn left onto FS 264 and drive 0.1 mile to a side road that forks to the left just before FS 264 fords the creek.

From the junction of GA 60 and US 76, drive south on GA 60 for 16.6 miles. Turn left onto Cooper Creek Road at the sign for Cooper Creek Recreation Area and follow the directions above.

GPS: N34 46.048 / W84 05.791

The Hike

The trail heads north up the logging road to the left of the creek. The old roadbed leads alongside a primitive campsite. Continue upstream to where the roadbed ends and a narrow dirt path leads uphill and veers off to the right. Follow this path, which soon dead-ends at the creek just downstream from Sea Creek Falls.

Sea Creek Falls is located within the Cooper Creek Scenic Area. Comprising 1,240 acres, the area has seventeen primitive campsites and is popular among hikers and mountain bikers. The coldwater creek is stocked on a regular basis, perhaps making the area best known for its ample fishing.

▶ While the terms *sea* and *ocean* are often used interchangeably, they are not the same. Oceans are much larger, and seas are typically surrounded by land. The smallest ocean, the Arctic, encompasses over five million square miles; the largest sea, the Mediterranean, is not much more than a million square miles.

Sea Creek Falls

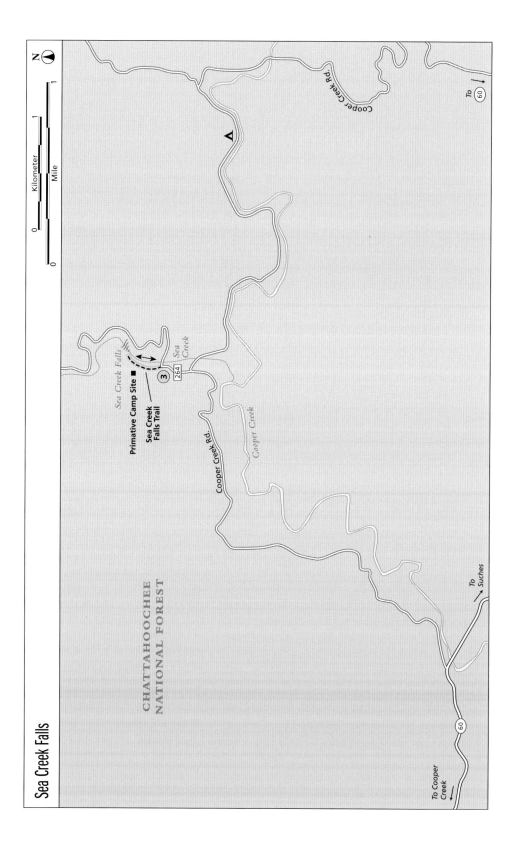

A mini mushroom forest grows on a dead tree stump.

Miles and Directions

0.0 From the trailhead, hike north up the old logging road. You soon come to a fork and bear right (northeast).

0.2 Pass a primitive campsite and continue east-northeast on the old roadbed. A short distance after the campsite, the trail starts to rise and bends right (east) toward the creek. Once you reach the creek, Sea Creek Falls is just upstream (N34 46.211 / W84 05.694). Return the way you came.

0.4 Arrive back at the trailhead.

4 Little Rock Creek Falls

Spirit filled! This falls feels old but not worn. Rather, it seems wise from age, as though all knowing.

Height: 50 feet
Beauty rating: Very good
Distance: 0.8 mile out and back
Difficulty: Moderate
Trail surface: Hard-packed dirt
Approximate hiking time: 40 minutes
Blaze color: No blazes

County: Fannin
Land status: National forest
Trail contact: Chattahoochee National Forest, Blue Ridge Ranger District; (706) 745-6928; www.fs.fed.us
Maps: *DeLorme: Georgia Atlas & Gazetteer:* Page 14 E5

Finding the trailhead: From the junction of GA 60 and GA 180, drive north on GA 60 for 11.7 miles. Turn left onto Rock Creek Road at the sign for the NATIONAL FOREST FISH HATCHERY and travel 3.2 miles to a small bridge. There are pull-offs on the left just before and just after the bridge.

From the junction of GA 60 and US 76, drive south on GA 60 for 15.6 miles. Turn right onto Rock Creek Road at the sign for the NATIONAL FOREST FISH HATCHERY and follow the directions above. The trailhead is located at the southeast side of the bridge.

(***Note:*** Rock Creek Road becomes unpaved at 1.1 miles.) GPS: N34 42.994 / W84 09.083

The Hike

A narrow path leads down from the trailhead and into the woods, following the creek south and upstream. As the trail rises and falls, it becomes very tough to navigate. Follow it as best you can, knowing that it stays within 100 feet of the creek at all times and continues to follow the creek upstream.

You will pass several small and lovely cascades along the way before arriving at the base of Little Rock Creek Falls. Be forewarned: Although this is not quite a full bushwhack, the very overgrown path is close to it.

While you are in the area, I recommend a visit to the nearby Chattahoochee National Forest Fish Hatchery. The hatchery proudly produces about 850,000 rainbow trout fingerlings per year. That's a lot of fish, and each one is raised with the sole purpose of restocking local Georgia waters.

▶ Rainbow trout appeal to both fly fishers and anglers. While the species isn't native to Georgia, it thrives here.

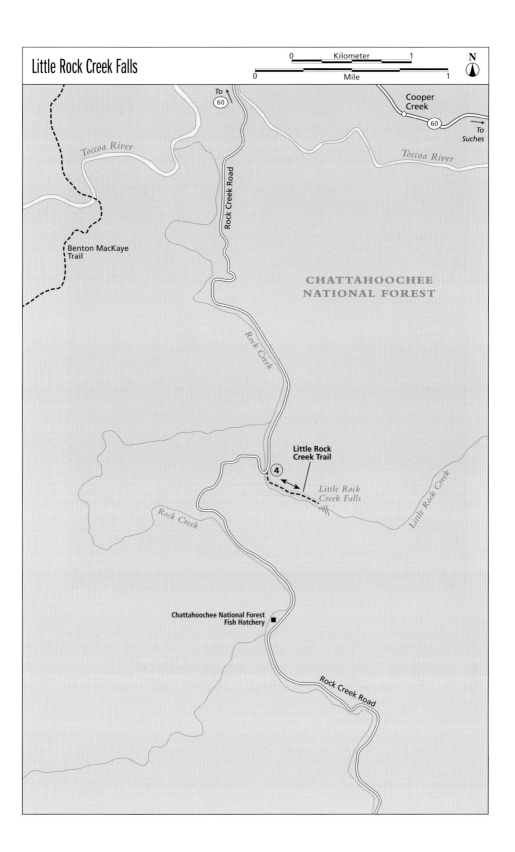

Little Rock Creek Falls

Kilometer
0   1
0   1
Mile

N

Toccoa River

To
60

Cooper
Creek

60

To
Suches

Toccoa River

Rock Creek Road

Benton MacKaye
Trail

CHATTAHOOCHEE
NATIONAL FOREST

Rock Creek

**Little Rock
Creek Trail**

4

*Little Rock
Creek Falls*

Little Rock Creek

Rock Creek

Chattahoochee National Forest
Fish Hatchery

Rock Creek Road

Bushwhack to the lively Little Rock Creek Falls.

Miles and Directions

0.0   From the trailhead, hike south on the narrow path as you follow the creek upstream.

0.4   Arrive at the base of Little Rock Creek Falls (N34 42.847 / W84 08.777). Return the way you came.

0.8   Arrive back at the trailhead.

5 Falls #1 on Waters Creek

Clean and neat! With its perfectly placed boulders and dazzling flow, Falls #1 on Waters Creek seems almost make-believe.

See map on page 26.
Height: 10 feet
Beauty rating: Excellent
Distance: 0.4 mile out and back
Difficulty: Easy
Trail surface: Hard-packed dirt
Approximate hiking time: 15 minutes
Blaze color: No blazes

County: Lumpkin
Land status: National forest
Trail contact: Chattahoochee National Forest, Chattooga Ranger District; (706) 754-6221; www.fs.fed.us
Maps: DeLorme: Georgia Atlas & Gazetteer: Page 15 F7

Finding the trailhead: From the junction of US 19 and US 129 at Turner's Corner, drive south on US 19 for 0.5 mile. Turn right onto Dicks Creek Road and travel 0.9 mile to a small parking area on the left.

From the junction of US 19 and GA 60 north, drive north on US 19 for 4.7 miles. Turn left onto Dicks Creek Road and follow the directions above.

The trailhead is located next to the information signpost across the street from the parking area. (**Note:** Dicks Creek Road becomes FS 34 after 2.2 miles.) GPS: N34 40.074/W83 55.205

The Hike

Follow the narrow footpath as it leads back toward the creek. Just before reaching the creek, head left (north) on the trail and follow the creek upstream. Less than 0.25 mile upstream, you will pass a bearing tree. A short distance past the bearing tree, arrive at the base of Falls #1 on Waters Creek.

Located within the Chestatee Wildlife Management Area, the land surrounding the falls is a playground for just about any outdoor enthusiast. Along with hikers, the area is frequented by equestrians and the occasional mountain biker. It is most popular, however, with local hunters and fishermen.

The short and easy hike to Falls #1 on Waters Creek offers high rewards.

Miles and Directions

0.0 From the trailhead at the information signpost, hike east on the narrow path toward the creek. Once at the creek, head left (north) and follow the creek upstream.

0.2 The narrow path brings you past a bearing tree and then leads to the base of Falls #1 on Waters Creek (N34 40.074 / W83 55.205). Return the way you came.

0.4 Arrive back at the trailhead.

6 Falls #2 on Waters Creek

Heavenly! Like its downstream sister, Falls #2 on Waters Creek is picture perfect. Lively and strong, this one keeps your attention. A popular swimming hole with the locals, it's a great place to cool off from the heat of a sunny day.

Height: 20 feet
Beauty rating: Excellent
Distance: Roadside
Difficulty: Easy
Blaze color: No blazes
County: Lumpkin
Land status: National forest
Trail contact: Chattahoochee National Forest,
Chattooga Ranger District; (706) 754-6221;
www.fs.fed.us
FYI: Open 7 a.m. to 10 p.m., with a nominal day-use fee; restrooms and trash cans at parking area
Maps: *DeLorme: Georgia Atlas & Gazetteer:* Page 15 E7

Finding the trailhead: From the junction of US 19 and US 129 at Turner's Corner, drive south on US 19 for 0.5 mile. Turn right onto Dicks Creek Road and travel 2.8 miles to a right turn into the parking area. From the parking area, head southwest across FS 34 and take one of the many short paths that lead to the base of Falls #2 on Waters Creek.

From the junction of US 19 and GA 60 north, drive north on US 19 for 4.7 miles. Turn left onto Dicks Creek Road and follow the directions above.

(***Note:*** Dicks Creek Road becomes FS 34 after 2.2 miles.) GPS: N34 40.743 / W83 56.178

Falls #2 on Waters Creek remains pure, despite the amount of traffic it sees.

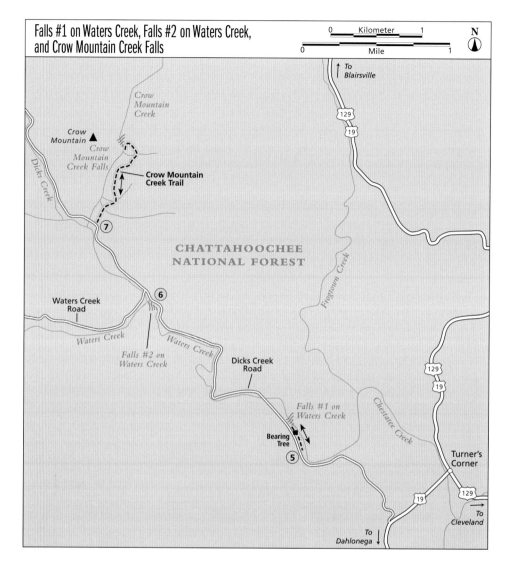

0   Kilometer   1

0   Mile   1

N

To
Blairsville

Crow
Mountain
Creek

129

19

Crow
Mountain ▲

Crow
Mountain
Creek Falls

Dicks Creek

Crow Mountain
Creek Trail

7

CHATTAHOOCHEE
NATIONAL FOREST

Frogtown Creek

Waters Creek
Road

6

Waters Creek

Waters Creek

Falls #2 on
Waters Creek

Dicks Creek
Road

129

19

Falls #1 on
Waters Creek

Chestatee Creek

Bearing
Tree

5

Turner's
Corner

19

129

To
Cleveland

To
Dahlonega

The Hike

Although the falls are visible from the road, to really appreciate them, take the very short walk from the parking area down to the base of Falls #2 on Waters Creek.

Many activities can be enjoyed within the Waters Creek Recreation Area. There's a very small campground with only eight primitive campsites, but they are pristine sites right along the creek's edge. The creek is considered one of Georgia's trophy trout streams. However, be sure to check out the state fishing regulations before you break out your pole and your waders.

▶ **State of Georgia fishing regulations can be found at the Georgia Department of Natural Resources website (www.gadnr.org) or by visiting www.georgiawildlife.com.**

7 Crow Mountain Creek Falls

Balanced! From the base of Crow Mountain Creek Falls, the balance of nature comes to mind. Tucked away deep in the forest, the creek makes its way down the mountainside until finally showing itself like a wonderful unexpected gift.

See map on page 26.
Height: 35 feet
Beauty rating: Good
Distance: 1.6 miles out and back
Difficulty: Moderate to strenuous
Trail surface: Wide old logging road and narrow hard-packed dirt
Approximate hiking time: 1 hour
Other trail users: Equestrians

Blaze color: No blazes
County: Lumpkin
Land status: National forest
Trail contact: Chattahoochee National Forest, Chattooga Ranger District; (706) 754-6221; www.fs.fed.us
Maps: *DeLorme: Georgia Atlas & Gazetteer:* Page 15 E7

Finding the trailhead: From the junction of US 19 and US 129 at Turner's Corner, drive south on US 19 for 0.5 mile. Turn right onto Dicks Creek Road and travel 3.5 miles to a pull-off on the right in front of an old logging road blocked by some dirt mounds.

From the junction of US 19 and GA 60 north, drive north on US 19 for 4.7 miles. Turn left onto Dicks Creek Road and follow the directions above.

The trailhead is located at the foot of the logging road. (***Note:*** Dicks Creek Road becomes FS 34 after 2.2 miles.) GPS: N34 41.201 / W83 56.601

The Hike

Begin by hiking over the mounds and following the old logging road uphill and into the forest. The trail soon brings you across a small tributary and then makes a short detour around some downed trees.

Beyond the downed trees, the trail continues to follow the old roadbed uphill, leading you across a second small tributary. As you continue hiking, the wide trail narrows to a footpath. The trail continues to alternately widen and narrow as it makes its way uphill to a side trail that forks off to the right (east). Bypass this trail and instead head left (north-northwest) and cross a third small tributary.

Continue your ascent a short distance farther to an obscure side trail that leads south to the brink of the falls. From the brink, *carefully* follow the creek downstream (south-southeast); it soon leads to the base of Crow Mountain Creek Falls.

Crow Mountain Creek flows from Crow Mountain and lies within the heart of the Chestatee Wildlife Management Area. Chestatee comes from the Cherokee word *a-tsv-sta-ti-yi,* meaning "firelight place." A popular means of hunting was to set a fire and flush wildlife toward the river, where they could be easily killed. The WMA is still popular with hunters, but nowadays they obviously use different means. Many other

If you keep your eyes peeled, you can often spot treasures like this wild turkey feather lying in the trail. Admire it, then leave it for others to enjoy.

recreational activities are enjoyed here, including hiking, birding, horseback riding, and fishing in the superb trout waters of Crow Mountain Creek.

Miles and Directions

0.0 From the trailhead, follow the old logging road north-northeast, uphill and into the forest.

0.1 Cross a small tributary and continue on a small side trail north-northwest around some downed trees. Once around the trees, continue following the old logging road.

0.2 Cross a second small tributary. Continue hiking north, deeper into the forest.

0.6 A side trail forks off to the right (east). Bypass this trail and stay left, following the main trail to a third small tributary. Cross it and continue hiking north-northwest.

0.7 Reach a side trail that leads south to the brink of the falls. Once at the brink, carefully follow the creek downstream (south-southeast).

0.8 Arrive at the base of Crow Mountain Creek Falls (N34 41.623 / W83 56.382). Return the way you came.

1.6 Arrive back at the trailhead.

8 Little Ridge Creek Falls

Triple threat! Get three times the pleasure from one trail! The Little Ridge Creek Trail offers three wonderful waterfalls, each having its own unique characteristics. Although this trail can be a bit hard to follow, if you make the effort you'll find these falls well worth the visit.

Height: Falls #1, 15 feet; Falls #2, 25 feet; Falls #3, 10 feet

Beauty rating: Falls #1, very good; Falls #2, good; Falls #3, excellent

Distance: 1.4 miles out and back

Difficulty: Moderate

Trail surface: Wide old logging road; obscure, hard-packed dirt trail

Approximate hiking time: 1 hour

Blaze color: No blazes

County: Lumpkin

Land status: National forest

Trail contact: Chattahoochee National Forest, Chattooga Ranger District; (706) 754-6221; www.fs.fed.us

FYI: Open 6 a.m. to 10 p.m.; nominal day-use fee

Maps: *DeLorme: Georgia Atlas and Gazetteer:* Page 15 E8

Finding the trailhead: From the junction of GA 129 and GA 180 east, drive south on GA 129 for 11.5 miles. Turn left onto unmarked FS 443 and travel 1.8 miles (be sure to stay left at both forks in the road) to just before the road fords the creek next to a small wooden footbridge. You will see a small parking area on the left in front of an old logging road.

From the junction of GA 129 and GA 19 at Turner's Corner, drive north on GA 129 for 1.35 miles. Turn right onto unmarked FS 443 at the sign for Bogg's Creek, and follow the directions above.

The trailhead is located where you parked at the base of the old logging road. (**Note:** If the parking area is full, backtrack 0.1 mile on FS 443 to another day-use parking area on the opposite side of the road.) GPS: N34 41.989 / W83 53.175

The Hike

Begin by hiking over the road-blocking mounds and following the wide old logging road north–northwest, uphill and upstream. The trail takes you across two small tributaries and then continues to follow Little Ridge Creek upstream. About 100 feet after you cross the second small tributary, a faint footpath leads to the creek. Take this footpath and cross the creek.

Head uphill for a short distance and pick up a very obscure trail that heads left (north) and continues to follow the creek upstream. Along the way you will pass some small cascades before coming to the first waterfall along the trail. A steep scramble to the bank takes you to the base of Falls #1 on Little Ridge Creek.

Little Ridge Creek Falls and DeSoto Falls

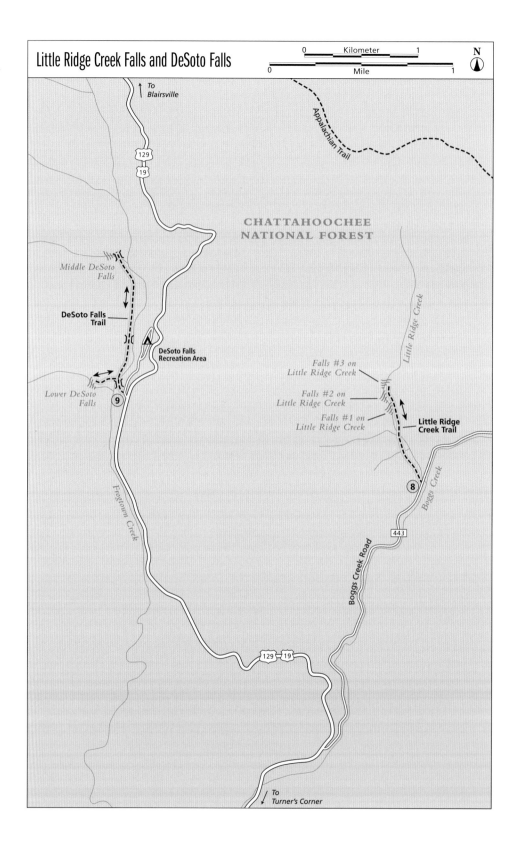

Kilometer

Mile

N

To
Blairsville

129
19

Appalachian Trail

CHATTAHOOCHEE
NATIONAL FOREST

Little Ridge Creek

Middle DeSoto
Falls

DeSoto Falls
Trail

DeSoto Falls
Recreation Area

Falls #3 on
Little Ridge Creek

Falls #2 on
Little Ridge Creek

Lower DeSoto
Falls

9

Falls #1 on
Little Ridge Creek

Little Ridge
Creek Trail

Frogtown Creek

Boggs Creek

8

443

Boggs Creek Road

129 — 19

To
Turner's Corner

Mountains in the distance wait to be explored.

Climb back up to the main trail and continue hiking north for another 0.1 mile. You soon arrive at the second and larger waterfall. Another steep scramble takes you down to the base of Falls #2 on Little Ridge Creek.

Third time's a charm! My personal favorite on this trail is the final waterfall that you come to, Falls #3. To reach it, climb back up to the main trail from Falls #2 and continue hiking north. Follow the trail until it dead-ends at the base of Falls #3 on Little Ridge Creek.

The story here lies behind the famous "Turner's Corner." While writing the driving directions, it dawned on me how many times I've passed it, referred to it, and yet never knew the story behind Turner's Corner. So after a bit of homework, here it is.

The famous Turner's Corner Cafe was established in 1928. In the years before, however, the cafe was the site of a gas station built in the early 1900s and owned by Mr. Turner. Unfortunately the sleepy location didn't see much business, so Mr. Turner had a brainstorm. He bought a black bear and trained it to dance. Some say he and the bear would sit in rocking chairs on the porch and wave to passersby. Naturally business improved, and to this day, the place is still known as Turner's Corner.

Miles and Directions

0.0 From the trailhead, hike north-northwest over the road-blocking mounds and follow the old logging road uphill and upstream.

0.1 The trail crosses a small tributary and then continues north-northwest upstream.

0.3 Cross a second small tributary and continue to hike north-northwest. About 100 feet after crossing this tributary, follow a faint footpath on the right that leads to the creek.

0.4 Cross the creek and head uphill for a short distance. Pick up a very obscure trail that heads left (north) and continue to follow the creek upstream.

0.5 Pass some small cascades, and then arrive at the first waterfall along the trail. A steep scramble leads west to the creek at the base of Falls #1 on Little Ridge Creek (N34 42.333 / W83 53.352). Return to the main trail and continue hiking north as you follow the creek upstream.

0.6 Arrive at the second, larger waterfall. Another steep scramble takes you down to the base of Falls #2 on Little Ridge Creek (N34 42.380 / W83 53.392). Return to the main trail and continue hiking north as you follow the creek upstream.

0.7 The trail dead-ends at the base of Falls #3 on Little Ridge Creek (N34 42.426 / W83 53.390). Return the way you came.

1.4 Arrive back at the trailhead.

9 DeSoto Falls

Astonishing! Twice the pleasure here, with both the Lower and the Middle Falls of DeSoto Falls to visit on the same trail. Despite being only 30 feet tall, DeSoto's Lower Falls creates a lot of sound for a smaller waterfall. Like a younger child trying to speak up for itself, this one demands the attention it deserves.

See map on page 30.
Height: Lower Falls, 30 feet; Middle Falls, 90 feet
Beauty rating: Very good
Distance: 2.6 miles out and back
Difficulty: Moderate
Trail surface: Hard-packed dirt with a short section of paved road
Approximate hiking time: 1 hour, 15 minutes
Blaze color: No blazes
County: Lumpkin

Land status: National forest
Trail contact: Chattahoochee National Forest, Chattooga Ranger District; (706) 754-6221; www.fs.fed.us
USDA Forest Service DeSoto Falls Campground; (706) 745-6928
FYI: Recreation area is open 7 a.m. to 10 p.m.; small day-use fee
Maps: *DeLorme: Georgia Atlas & Gazetteer:* Page 15 E8

Finding the trailhead: From the junction of US 129 and GA 180 east, drive south on US 129 for 8.9 miles. Turn right into the DeSoto Falls Recreation Area at the sign and head down the hill. Take the first left into the large parking area.

From the junction of US 129 and US 19 at Turner's Corner, drive north on US 129 for 4.0 miles. Turn left at the sign into the DeSoto Falls Recreation Area and follow the directions above.

The trailhead is at the northwest corner of the parking area, next to the self-pay station and the restrooms. GPS: N34 42.395/W83 54.916

The Hike

Follow the wide gravel path past the restrooms and head into the picnic area. After passing through the picnic area, the trail leads you to a T junction at a paved road. Go left here, entering the campground. A short distance into the campground, you will see a wooden footbridge that heads over Frogtown Creek.

After crossing the footbridge, immediately come to a T junction. The left leads downstream toward Lower Falls; the right leads to Middle Falls. Head left and the trail takes you up and around several switchbacks for 0.3 mile to where it dead-ends at the base of Lower DeSoto Falls. Backtrack to the T and head the other way toward Middle Falls. While this is a longer trek, I personally feel that Middle Falls is worth the extra work.

Symmetrical and sophisticated, DeSoto's Middle Falls creates a perfectly planned path as it flows down the mountainside. From the T junction, follow the wide and well-maintained trail upstream. The relatively flat path meanders through the forest

HERNANDO DE SOTO: EXPLORER

Hernando de Soto was born sometime around the year 1500 in Spain. His parents were "hidalgos," Spanish nobles who did not hold a title. They lived modestly, and their status in society exempted them from paying taxes.

As de Soto grew from a boy to a young man, so did his ambitions, and in 1514 Hernando de Soto was off to explore the New World. Under the leadership of the governor of Panama, Pedrarias Davila, de Soto and hundreds of other men embarked on a journey across the ocean. This group proceeded to explore and conquer Central America.

During this conquest, Hernando de Soto gained a reputation as a brave leader, excellent horseman, and ruthless tactician. He soon had the confidence and leadership skills to guide his own explorations and headed out to find a passageway between the Atlantic and Pacific Oceans. If he could find such a passageway, he could open up a trade route between Spain and the riches of the Orient.

Failing to find a passage, de Soto sailed south. In 1530 he joined forces with Francisco Pizarro, who made him a captain in the Spanish army. De Soto played an active role in the Spanish conquest of the Inca in Peru. As a conquistador, or conqueror, de Soto returned to Spain a very wealthy man, with shiploads of gold and other treasure pillaged from the Inca.

De Soto's thirst for gold and glory never waned, and in 1537 he was granted permission by the King of Spain to conquer Florida. Although Florida had been discovered earlier by Juan Ponce de León, it had never been conquered, colonized, or ruled by Spain. So de Soto set sail once again, leading his own expedition with hundreds of soldiers, some priests, and ten ships across the ocean.

His party first landed in Cuba, and after conquering and governing it, de Soto and his men spent the next several months preparing for the invasion of Florida. They gathered soldiers, armor, equipment, and livestock prior to making their way north. In 1539, with nearly a thousand men and hundreds of horses at the ready, they embarked on the next leg of their journey to the western coast of Florida.

In Florida de Soto quickly gained the reputation of a brutal conqueror, savaging everything in his way. His explorations expanded throughout the Southeast, and he is credited as being the first European to explore west of the Mississippi River.

Hernando de Soto died in 1542. His remains are buried somewhere near the banks of the river he explored centuries ago.

Upper DeSoto Falls sits tucked away from the crowds.

and takes you to a small wooden footbridge. Cross the bridge and in a short distance you see some side trails on your right heading to the creek. Bypass these, continuing straight ahead (north) on the main unblazed trail.

The trail now begins to rise and fall before leading to another wooden footbridge. A short distance after crossing this one, a trail forks off to the left (west) and up. Take this left fork and follow the path west to where it dead-ends at the base of Middle DeSoto Falls.

Some of you may remember the time when you could also visit the Upper Falls here. The trail to Upper Falls, however, is now closed due to erosion. Once again, *this* is why we do not shortcut on trails.

DeSoto Falls Scenic Area is named for the Spanish explorer Hernando de Soto. Hernando was the first European to explore the interior of Georgia, which he did in the late 1530s. The falls got their name when some early settlers found a piece of armor near the falls and attributed the relic to de Soto and his men.

Miles and Directions

0.0 Follow the wide gravel path northwest into the picnic area. Head right (north) through the picnic area, passing more picnic tables.

0.1 Come to a T junction at a paved road. Go left (west) at the T and head into the campground.

0.2 Inside the campground, you will see a trail information sign and a wooden footbridge over the creek on the left. Cross the footbridge (north-northwest) and immediately come to a T junction. The right leads east to Middle Falls; the left leads west to Lower Falls. Go left (west) for now and follow Frogtown Creek downstream. The trail begins its ascent as it takes you around several switchbacks.

0.5 The trail dead-ends at the base of Lower DeSoto Falls (N34 42.440 / W83 55.061). Backtrack to the T at the footbridge over the creek.

0.8 Arrive back at the T, and hike straight ahead (east) toward the Middle DeSoto Falls, following the wide and well-maintained trail upstream.

1.0 Cross a small wooden footbridge and continue hiking north. Bypassing the side trails that lead to the creek, stay on the main path as the trail begins to rise and fall.

1.5 Cross another wooden footbridge and continue hiking northeast. Shortly after crossing this footbridge, follow the trail that forks off to the left (west) and up.

1.6 The trail dead-ends at the base of Middle DeSoto Falls (N34 43.017 / W83 54.934). Retrace your steps to the T junction at 0.8 mile.

2.4 Arrive back at the T junction, and go left (south) over the footbridge and return to the trailhead the way you came.

2.6 Arrive back at the trailhead.

10 Helton Creek Falls

Gorgeous! Helton Creek is a wonderful place to spend the day. This very short and easy trail takes you to two beautiful waterfalls. The Upper Falls is a popular hangout and swimming hole for the locals. So if its seclusion you seek, I suggest visiting these falls on a weekday to avoid the heavy traffic of weekend picnickers.

Height: Lower Falls, 30 feet; Upper Falls, 50 feet
Beauty rating: Excellent
Distance: 0.4 mile out and back
Difficulty: Easy
Trail surface: Hard-packed dirt
Approximate hiking time: 20 minutes

Blaze color: No blazes
County: Union
Land status: National forest
Trail contact: Chattahoochee National Forest, Chattooga Ranger District; (706) 754-6221; www.fs.fed.us Maps: *DeLorme: Georgia Atlas & Gazetteer:* Page 15 D8

Finding the trailhead: From the junction of US 129 and GA 180 east, drive south on US 129 for 3.7 miles. Turn left onto Helton Creek Road at the sign for HELTON CREEK FALLS and travel 2.2 miles to a large parking area on your right.

From the junction of US 129 and US 19 at Turner's Corner, drive north on US 129 for 9.2 miles. Turn right onto Helton Creek Road and follow the directions above.

The trailhead is located at the northwest end of the parking lot. GPS: N34 45.198 / W83 53.669

The Hike

Make your way down the log steps. The easily followed trail then bends left, crosses a small wooden footbridge, and leads to a set of stairs on the left that descend to the Lower Falls of Helton Creek. Flat rocks are plentiful, and peaceful creek views greet you at the base of this beauty.

From the Lower Falls get back on the main trail and continue a very short distance farther to the taller, more powerful, Upper Falls of Helton Creek. If you're brave enough to swim in the chilly creek waters, this is a wonderful place to do so. You can swim right under the strong flow of the falls at this one.

Located near Vogel State Park and in the heart of Union County, Helton Creek Falls sits in a prime location. The area offers hiking trails, mountain biking, and horseback riding for the outdoor enthusiast. If you prefer tamer activities, you could go shopping in Helen, check out the antiquing in Hiawassee, or try your hand at gem mining in the nearby town of Dahlonega. This area has it all.

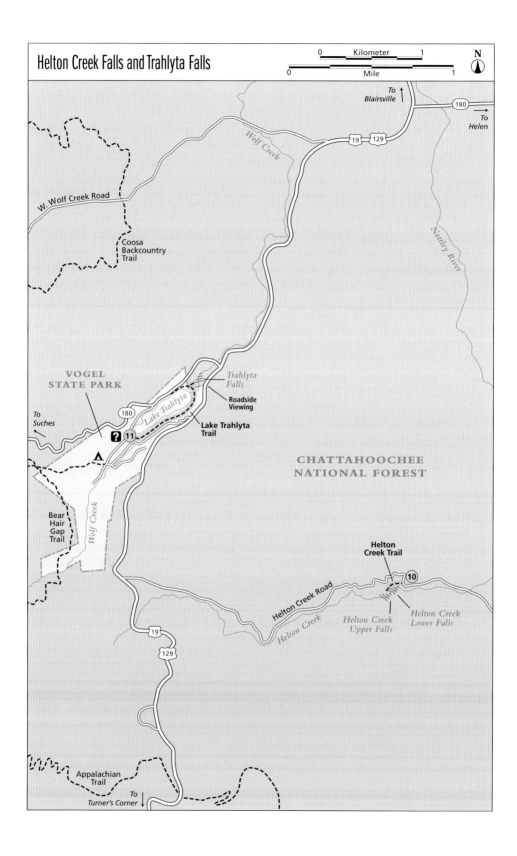

Helton Creek Falls and Trahlyta Falls

Kilometer
0 1

Mile
0 1

N

To
Blairsville

To
Helen

180

19 129

Wolf Creek

Nottley River

W. Wolf Creek Road

Coosa
Backcountry
Trail

VOGEL
STATE PARK

Trahlyta
Falls

Roadside
Viewing

Lake Trahlyta

Lake Trahlyta
Trail

To
Suches

180

11

CHATTAHOOCHEE
NATIONAL FOREST

Bear
Hair
Gap
Trail

Wolf Creek

Helton
Creek Trail

10

Helton Creek Road

Helton Creek
Upper Falls

Helton Creek
Lower Falls

Helton Creek

19

129

Appalachian
Trail

To
Turner's Corner

The short hike to Upper Helton Creek Falls sees a lot of traffic, but it's worth sharing.

Miles and Directions

0.0   From the trailhead, head down the steps and hike north-northwest on the narrow trail as it bends around and into the forest.

0.1   Come to a set of stairs on the left that leads east and down to the base of Helton Creek's Lower Falls (N34 45.193 / W83 53.712). Return to the main trail, continuing south on the narrow path.

0.2   Arrive at an observation deck at the base of the Upper Falls of Helton Creek (N34 45.162 / W83 53.744). Return the way you came.

0.4   Arrive back at the trailhead.

11 Trahlyta Falls

Lively! This one has spirit and spice and is sure to light up your day and bring a smile to your face. Although you can get a great view of Trahlyta Falls from the roadside, an easy lakeside hike will allow you literally to reach out and touch this one.

See map on page 38.
Height: 45 feet
Beauty rating: Excellent
Distance: Roadside or 1.5 miles out and back
Difficulty: Easy
Trail surface: Hard-packed dirt
Approximate hiking time: 40 minutes
Blaze color: No blazes

County: Union
Land status: State park
Trail contact: Vogel State Park; (706) 745-2628; www.gastateparks.org/Vogel
FYI: Open 7 a.m. to 10 p.m.; small day-use fee
Maps: *DeLorme: Georgia Atlas & Gazetteer:* Page 15 D7-D8

Finding the trailhead: *Roadside viewing:* From the junction of GA 129 and GA 180 east, drive south on GA 129 for 2.5 miles to a paved pull-off on the right.

From the junction of GA 129 and GA 19 at Turner's Corner, drive north on GA 129 for 10.5 miles to a paved pull-off on the left.

Lake Trahlyta Trail: From the junction of GA 129 and GA 180 east, drive south on GA 129 for 2.6 miles. Turn right into Vogel State Park and head down the hill for 0.4 mile. As soon as you cross the small bridge over the creek, you will see a large parking area on the right next to the lake.

From the junction of GA 129 and GA 19 at Turner's Corner, drive north on GA 129 for 10.3 miles. Turn left into Vogel State Park and follow the directions above.

The trailhead is located at the southeast end of the parking lot at the LAKE TRAHLYTA TRAIL sign. GPS: N34 45.957 / W83 55.391

The Hike

Trahlyta Falls can be viewed from the roadside, or you can enjoy a lovely hike along Lake Trahlyta to get a more personal feel for the falls.

The trail begins by leading you across a footbridge over Wolf Creek. The trail then heads left and passes a picnic pavilion. The easily followed path follows the lakeside a short distance until you come to a fork. You can take either path here—they reunite less than 0.1 mile farther along the trail.

Continue to follow the lake's edge until you reach a bridge at the far east end of the lake. Cross the bridge and immediately look to the right for a side trail heading downhill. This is the Falls Bottom Trail. Take this side trail as it makes its way steeply down to an observation deck at the base of Trahlyta Falls. The falls come alive from the base as they freely fall within arm's reach.

Lake Trahlyta can be serene just after sunrise.

Lake Trahlyta was created in the 1930s by the Civilian Conservation Corps, and the lake and falls were named for Indian Princess Trahlyta.

In the years before white settlers came to live here, great battles occurred between the Creek and Cherokee tribes. It is said that the creeks would run red with blood, and the mountains of Blood and Slaughter were named in tribute to the battles' ferocity.

During this wartime, Princess Trahlyta was kidnapped by a suitor she had rejected. She died in captivity and is buried south of the park, near the junction of US 19 and GA 60 at Stonepile Gap.

Miles and Directions

0.0 From the trailhead, cross the footbridge over Wolf Creek and head left (east). The wide, easily followed path follows the edge of the lake.

0.2 The trail splits. Take either path as you continue to hike along the lake's edge.

0.3 The trails merge together again. Continue hiking east along the lake.

0.6 Cross a bridge at the far east end of the lake. Immediately after crossing the bridge, you will see the Falls Bottom Trail on the right. Follow the Falls Bottom Trail northeast and down toward the falls.

0.75 Arrive at an observation deck alongside Trahlyta Falls (N34 46.190 / W83 54.989). Return the way you came.

1.5 Arrive back at the trailhead.

LEGEND OF PRINCESS TRAHLYTA

Princess Trahlyta was said to have been a true nature lover. She would walk the mountain trails and revel in the splendor of the forest. According to legend, she would sip of the springs, which had a magical power that kept her youthful.

When Princess Trahlyta was kidnapped by the Cherokee warrior Wahsega, he took her far from the safe haven of her mountain home. They say it was her lack of freedom in the forest that killed her, not an act of violence.

According to folklore, passersby who tossed a stone upon her grave would be blessed with good health and good fortune. If you pass her grave today, you'll see that it is plainly marked by a large pile of stones near Stonepile Gap.

12 Raven Cliffs Falls

Unique! Raven Cliffs Falls is unlike any other waterfall in the area. A captivating mystery, it is fed by two streams that appear to come right out of the mountain and then plunge perfectly between the cliffs into the grotto below.

Height: 50 feet
Beauty rating: Excellent
Distance: 4.8 miles out and back
Difficulty: Easy to moderate
Trail surface: Hard-packed dirt
Approximate hiking time: 2 hours, 20 minutes
Blaze color: No blazes

County: White
Land status: National forest
Trail contact: Chattahoochee National Forest, Chattooga Ranger District; (706) 754-6221; www.fs.fed.us
Maps: *DeLorme: Georgia Atlas & Gazetteer:* Page 15 E9

Finding the trailhead: From the junction of GA 75 Alternate and GA 75 (just north of Helen), drive west on GA 75A for 2.25 miles. Turn right onto GA 348 (Richard B. Russell Scenic Highway) and travel 2.6 miles to a left turn onto FS 244 at the sign for RAVEN CLIFFS RECREATION AREA. Head down the hill and go over a small bridge to the parking area on the left.

From the junction of GA 348 and GA 180, drive south on GA 348 for 11.2 miles. Turn right onto FS 244 at the sign for RAVEN CLIFFS RECREATION AREA and follow the directions above.

The trailhead is located next to the bridge. GPS: N34 42.593 / W83 47.354

The Hike

Walk back west toward the bridge from the parking area; the trailhead is just before the bridge on your left.

The Raven Cliffs Falls Trail (#22) heads up a few wooden steps and off into the woods. The well-groomed and easy-to-follow trail leads to a footbridge. Cross the bridge and continue enjoying the wonderful hike, heading upstream along the creek. You pass two beautiful waterfalls along the way before going up and over a rise and arriving at some wooden planks. Cross these and find yourself on an island where the creek splits and surrounds you. Continue following the trail and cross another log footbridge, putting you back on the bank of the creek.

After strolling through the forest for less than 0.5 mile more, come to a third amazing waterfall in the creek. Continue on the trail as it makes a slow, steady climb to yet a fourth wondrous treasure of a waterfall. Don't be fooled by these beauties— the main attraction is yet to come and well worth the hike.

Continue following the trail upstream and across another log footbridge. You soon come to a fork in the trail before crossing yet another log footbridge. The trail rises and falls until you reach a tiny tributary. Rock-hop across it and then pass through an

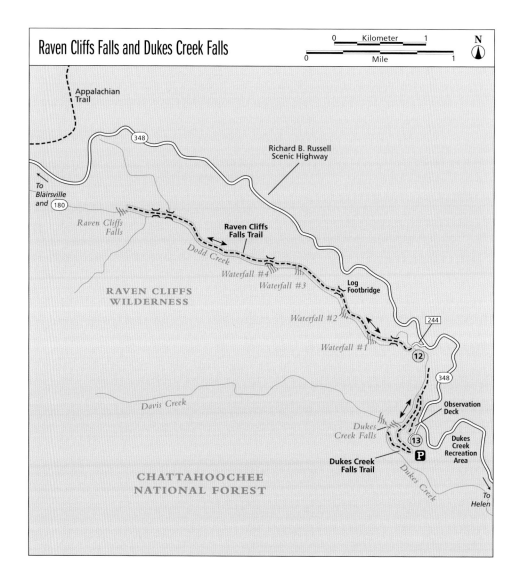

Kilometer

Mile

N

Appalachian Trail

348

Richard B. Russell Scenic Highway

To Blairsville and 180

Raven Cliffs Falls

Raven Cliffs Falls Trail

Dodd Creek

RAVEN CLIFFS WILDERNESS

Waterfall #4

Waterfall #3

Log Footbridge

Waterfall #2

244

Waterfall #1

12

348

Davis Creek

Observation Deck

Dukes Creek Falls

13

Dukes Creek Recreation Area

P

Dukes Creek Falls Trail

Dukes Creek

CHATTAHOOCHEE NATIONAL FOREST

To Helen

open primitive camping area. Past the camping area, the trail becomes evident again. Cross two more footbridges and rock-hop another small tributary before arriving at a fork in the trail. Bear right at the fork and make your final, steep ascent to a view of the cliffs in the distance. Climb up the rocky, muddy path to the boulders at the base of the cliffs. Raven Cliffs Falls comes pouring down between the cliffs.

Once at Raven Cliffs, you could continue on the trail to the right of the cliffs for views of the surrounding mountains from atop the cliffs, as well as another 100-foot waterfall, which is not visible from the base. This trail is very steep, slippery, and *dangerous*. To reach the top of the cliffs you must first climb the muddy slope and then traverse a 40-foot section of tree roots. Immediately after climbing the tree roots,

Raven Cliffs Falls pours out of the mountain between the cliffs that loom above.

there is a large hole that could easily kill anyone who accidentally fell inside. There are no guardrails or man-made boundaries of any sort at the top of the cliffs, and the drop-offs are very steep and very high.

I do not advise hiking to the top. However, if you choose to do so, *use extreme caution!* This portion of the hike should be attempted by experienced hikers only.

Located within the Raven Cliffs Wilderness, for most of the hike the trail closely follows Dodd Creek, named for Ed Dodd, an environmentalist, national park guide, and creator of the *Mark Trail* comic strip. Once a popular place for rappelling, this activity was banned in 1986 to protect the cliffs from erosion.

THE AMAZING SALAMANDER

Salamanders are frequently seen at the base of Raven Cliffs Falls. These passive amphibians have a range that covers the world over. They can be found on every continent except for Antarctica. Some species can grow to be 6 feet long and weigh up to 140 pounds. No need to fear, you won't find these giant salamander species anywhere near the pool at Raven Cliffs. Most species, including those found here, rarely exceed 6 inches.

Salamanders' smooth, slick skin must remain moist at all times or they can die. This explains their presence in the cool mountain water below the falls. Humans are salamanders' worst enemy and the number-one reason for their demise. If you see one along the banks or pools of a mountain stream, please let it be and observe it from afar—perhaps through the lens of a camera so that others can one day see it too.

Miles and Directions

0.0 From the trailhead, the trail heads west, up some wooden steps and off into the woods.

0.2 Come to a footbridge. Cross it and continue hiking northwest as the trail follows the creek upstream.

0.3 Pass the first of four wonderful waterfalls on your way to Raven Cliffs. Continue hiking west along the creek's edge.

0.6 Pass a second beautiful waterfall; continue hiking north and upstream.

0.7 The trail crosses wooden planks onto a small island where the creek splits around you. Continue north-northwest on the island to reach a log footbridge back to the bank.

1.0 Pass a third amazing waterfall. Continue to follow the creek west as the trail makes a slow and steady climb.

1.2 Hike past a fourth, wondrous treasure of a waterfall as you make your way deeper into the forest. Continue hiking north-northwest along the creek's edge.

1.3 Cross another footbridge and continue hiking southwest.

1.4 Come to a fork. Stay to the left (west) at the fork and cross some logs. Continue hiking as the trail rises and falls and brings you across another tributary. Rock-hop across it as you make your way further into the wilderness.

1.7 Pass through an open primitive camping area, continuing west. The trail becomes evident again on the other side.

2.0 Cross a footbridge and continue hiking west.

2.1 Cross another footbridge; once again, continue hiking west.

2.3 Reach another fork in the trail. Go right to make a final steep ascent as the cliffs come into view in the distance.

2.4 Climb up the rocky, muddy path to the boulders at the base of Raven Cliffs Falls (N34 43.402 / W83 49.410). Return the way you came.

4.8 Arrive back at the trailhead.

13 Dukes Creek Falls

Fire and ice! Meeting with a fury, these two creeks crash together in the most tremendous way! I assure you, photos do no justice to these beauties. Sitting side by side, two wonderful waterfalls come together to create Dukes Creek Falls.

See map on page 44.
Height: 250 feet
Beauty rating: Excellent
Distance: 2.2 miles out and back
Difficulty: Moderate
Trail surface: Hard-packed dirt; sections of wooden boardwalk; portion is wheelchair accessible
Approximate hiking time: 1 hour
Blaze color: Green

County: White
Land status: National forest
Trail contact: Chattahoochee National Forest, Chattooga Ranger District; (706) 754-6221; www.fs.fed.us
FYI: Open 7 a.m. to 10 p.m.; small day-use fee; primitive bathroom, ample trash cans in parking area
Maps: *DeLorme: Georgia Atlas & Gazetteer:* Page 15 E9

Finding the trailhead: From the junction of GA 75 Alternate and GA 75 (just north of Helen), drive west on GA 75A for 2.25 miles. Turn right onto GA 348 (Richard B. Russell Scenic Highway) and travel 1.6 miles to a left turn into Dukes Creek Recreation Area.

From the junction of GA 348 and GA 180, drive south on GA 348 for 12.1 miles. Turn right into the Dukes Creek Recreation Area.

The trailhead is located at the south side of the parking area. GPS: N34 42.105 / W83 47.373

The Hike

A paved path leads downhill for 0.1 mile to an observation deck with a view of Dukes Creek Falls in the far distance. This portion of the trail is wheelchair accessible. If you've got binoculars you can get an okay view of the falls from here. However, to truly experience the power and might of these falls, a hike to the base is necessary.

To get to the base from the observation deck, continue along the wooden path and make your way down into the forest on a wide trail. The easily followed path takes you to another wooden boardwalk and down two sets of steps to a T junction. Go left at the T and follow the main trail as it makes a very slow descent, following the creek downstream.

Along the creek's edge you are treated to a lovely small waterfall and many lively cascades before the trail brings you to a hard switchback to the right. Follow the switchback around; the trail now begins to make a steeper descent before taking you to one last wooden boardwalk. This one leads to the observation decks at the base of Dukes Creek Falls.

Davis and Dodd Creeks meet to create Dukes Creek Falls.

I urge you not to shortcut here! So many people have done so in the past that the resulting erosion is killing the surrounding flora and fauna.

It is said that the great Georgia gold rush began along Dukes Creek back in 1828. Credit has been given to Fred Logan, although it is quite possible that one of his slaves actually made the find. Whoever discovered it stirred the beginning of the first significant gold rush in U.S. history.

Red-tailed hawks are one of the most common hawks in North America and feed primarily on small mammals.

Miles and Directions

0.0   From the trailhead, the paved path leads downhill and west.

0.1   Arrive at an observation deck. Dukes Creek Falls can be seen in the distance. Continue north along the wooden boardwalk.

0.3   Head down some steps and come to a T junction. Go left (southwest) at the T; the trail follows the creek downstream from high above.

0.8   The trail makes a hard switchback to the right (west). Follow it around the switchback as you begin to make a steeper descent.

1.1   Arrive at an observation deck at the base of Dukes Creek Falls (N34 42.128/W83 47.521). Return the way you came.

2.2   Arrive back at the trailhead.

14 Horse Trough Falls

Wondrous! Horse Trough Falls truly makes you wonder how such a tiny creek at the top could feed such a massive waterfall and then in an instant become, once again, a simple little forest stream. Nature certainly is amazing. This one is recommended for hikers of all ages and abilities.

Height: 70 feet
Beauty rating: Very good
Distance: 0.2 mile out and back
Difficulty: Easy
Trail surface: Wide gravel
Approximate hiking time: 10 minutes
Blaze color: Green
County: Union

Land status: National forest
Trail contact: Chattahoochee National Forest, Chattooga Ranger District; (706) 754-6221; www.fs.fed.us
FYI: Open 7 a.m. to 10 p.m.
Maps: DeLorme: Georgia Atlas & Gazetteer: Page 15 D9

Finding the trailhead: From the junction of GA 75 and GA 356, drive north on GA 75 for 8.4 miles. Turn left onto FS 44 at the gray sign for Mark Wilderness Trail and travel 4.5 miles to a right turn into the Upper Chattahoochee River Campground. Drive into the campground and pass the bathhouse. The road bends a little to the left with a sign for Horse Trough Falls. Follow the bend, and the signs, until the road dead-ends at a turnaround. You will see a sign on the right for day-use parking.

From the junction of GA 75 and GA 180, drive south on GA 75 for 2.5 miles. Turn right onto FS 44 at the brown sign for the Chattahoochee National Forest Wildlife Management Area and follow the directions above.

The trailhead is located at the north-northwest end of the parking area and is marked with a sign for Trail #173. GPS: N34 47.521 / W83 47.119

The Hike

Follow the wide gravel trail as it leads into the woods and over a footbridge. You will pass several information posts along the way for a self-guided tour of the forest. The short, easy-to-follow path soon leads to an observation deck at the base of Horse Trough Falls.

Horse Trough Falls

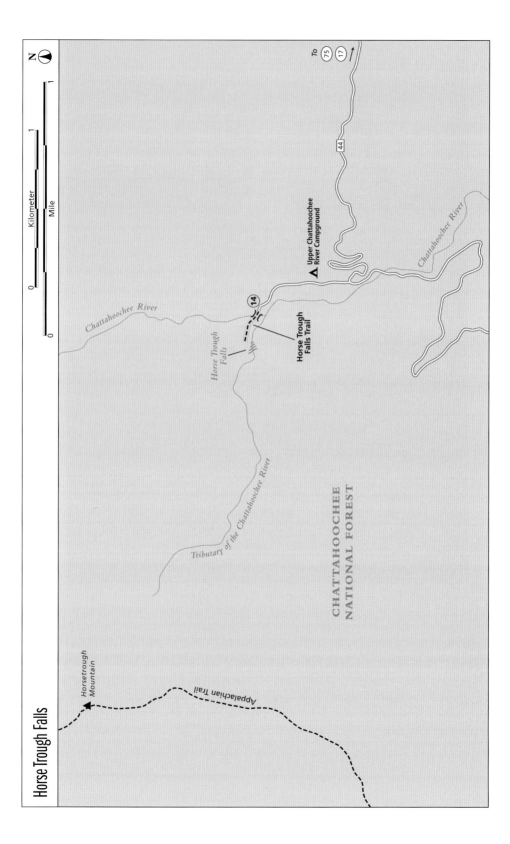

Horsetrough Mountain

Appalachian Trail

Tributary of the Chattahoochee River

CHATTAHOOCHEE NATIONAL FOREST

Horse Trough Falls

Chattahoochee River

Horse Trough Falls Trail

14

Upper Chattahoochee River Campground

44

Chattahoochee River

To 75 17

N

Kilometer
0   1
Mile
0   1

Horse Trough Falls sits off in the distance.

Named for and flowing from Horsetrough Mountain, the falls and mountain are located within the Mark Trail Wilderness. Oddly enough, Mark Trail is a fictional character from a comic strip that was first penned in 1946. The character was a photo-journalist and magazine writer who quelled the evils of those doing ecological and environmental misdeeds. Well before his time, he would have fit right into today's eco-friendly society.

THE ORIGINS OF SUPERMAN

Well before the time of Mark Trail, the first comic books in the United States appeared in the 1800s. These first "proto" comic books were books containing collections of newspaper comic strips, such as the *Famous Funnies*. It wasn't until 1938 that Action Comics #1 introduced us to Superman, arguably the most famous superhero in America.

Created by Jerry Siegel and Joe Shuster, the "man of steel" went on to be not only a superhero but also a superstar. He had a long-running comic book series, a radio show, a television series, and several blockbuster movies.

Miles and Directions

0.0 From the trailhead, follow the wide gravel trail north and into the woods. Cross a footbridge and pass several information signposts along the way.

0.1 Arrive at the base of Horse Trough Falls (N34 47.555 / W83 47.200). Return the way you came.

0.2 Arrive back at the trailhead.

15 High Shoals Falls

Twice the treat! The High Shoals Trail offers two incredible waterfalls. The first treat is the Blue Hole. In a word . . . Inviting! The waters of the Blue Hole open their arms to you and inspire you to spend an afternoon picnicking and basking in their delight. The Lower Falls at High Shoals is yet to come. Like the talons of an eagle catching its prey, the water here clings to the rock as it swoops down the mountainside.

Height: Blue Hole, 25 feet; Lower Falls, 100 feet
Beauty rating: Excellent
Distance: 2.4 miles out and back
Difficulty: Moderate to strenuous
Trail surface: Hard-packed dirt
Approximate hiking time: 1 hour, 30 minutes
Blaze color: Green

County: Towns
Land status: National park
Trail contact: Chattahoochee National Forest, Blue Ridge Ranger District; (706) 745-6928; www.fs.fed.us
Maps: DeLorme: Georgia Atlas & Gazetteer: Page 15 C9

Finding the trailhead: From the junction of GA 75 and GA 356, drive north on GA 75 for 10.4 miles. Turn right onto Indian Grave Gap Road (FS 283) at the sign for HIGH SHOALS and travel 1.3 miles to the small parking area on the left next to some trash cans.

From the junction of GA 75 and GA 180, drive south on GA 75 for 0.5 mile. Turn left onto Indian Grave Gap Road (FS 283) at the sign for HIGH SHOALS and follow the directions above.

The trailhead for High Shoals Trail (#19) is located at the north end of the parking area. (**Note:** Indian Grave Gap Road fords a small creek. On days when water levels are high, you may need a high-clearance vehicle to ford the creek.) GPS: N34 48.968 / W83 43.626

The Hike

From the trailhead, take the steps down into the woods and onto the well-maintained, easily followed trail. The trail continues to descend until you reach a post sticking out of the ground with a missing sign. At this post, you will see a narrow trail heading straight ahead and the wider main trail that turns to the right. Go right here, following the main trail as it continues its descent toward the forest floor.

When you finally reach the forest floor, go left (north), following the wide High Shoals

▶ The bald eagle was adopted as the national bird of the United States of America in 1782 and to this day stands as a symbol of freedom. These regal eagles have a wingspan of up to 8 feet. Now that's impressive.

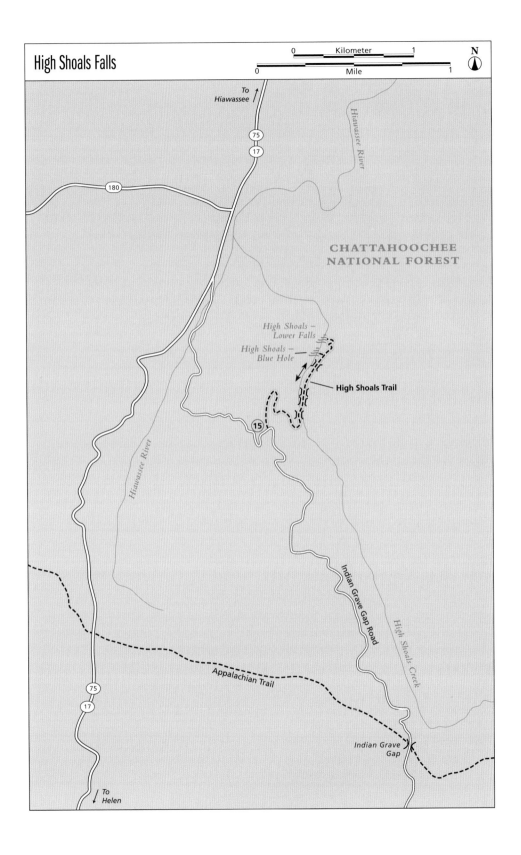

High Shoals Falls

0 — Kilometer — 1
0 — Mile — 1

N

To
Hiawassee

75
17

180

Hiawassee River

CHATTAHOOCHEE
NATIONAL FOREST

High Shoals –
Lower Falls

High Shoals –
Blue Hole

High Shoals Trail

15

Hiawassee River

Indian Grave Gap Road

High Shoals Creek

Appalachian Trail

75
17

Indian Grave
Gap

To
Helen

High Shoals Falls clings to the rocky mountainside.

Trail. Enjoy a flat forest stroll alongside the creek until you come to a wooden foot-bridge. Cross it, and head left. Three more footbridges/log planks follow. After crossing the last of them, head downhill and you will see, and hear, the falls on your left. A side trail makes a sharp left switchback to an observation deck at the base of Blue Hole Falls.

After enjoying the Blue Hole, head back up to the main trail and continue to the Lower Falls. The trail continues its descent into the forest and around some switchbacks until you arrive at the observation deck at the base of the High Shoals Lower Falls.

The High Shoals Scenic Area that is home to these wonderful waterfalls covers 170 acres. There are actually five falls in succession along the creek, but in an effort to protect the area, I have chosen to include only those with maintained trails.

Indian Grave Gap Road, your access road, was named for Indian Grave Gap, which sits at 3,120 feet. Given the history of this area, there's a good chance it was aptly named.

Miles and Directions

0.0 From the trailhead, take the steps north, down into the woods.

0.2 Come to a junction marked by a post sticking out of the ground. A narrow trail heads straight ahead; the wider main trail turns to the right. Go right (south) here and continue following the High Shoals Trail downhill.

0.6 Enjoy the stroll along the forest floor before coming to a footbridge. Cross the bridge and continue north as you pass a primitive campsite.

0.7 Cross a second and third footbridge as you continue to hike north.

0.9 After crossing a fourth footbridge, hike northeast down the hill until you see and hear the falls on your left.

1.0 A side trail makes a hard switchback to the left (west) and takes you down to an observation deck at the base of Blue Hole Falls (N34 49.292 / W83 43.331). From Blue Hole, head back up to the main trail and continue hiking northwest deeper into the forest. The trail descends as it leads around some switchbacks.

1.2 Arrive at the base of High Shoals Lower Falls (N34 49.353 / W83 43.309). Return the way you came.

2.4 Arrive back at the trailhead.

16 Anna Ruby Falls

Showy! Located adjacent to Unicoi State Park, Anna Ruby Falls is one of the most frequently visited waterfalls in the area. Although overcrowded, the falls are quite beautiful and worth a visit. Don't expect seclusion here, and you won't be disappointed.

Height: 153 feet and 50 feet
Beauty rating: Excellent
Distance: 0.8 mile out and back
Difficulty: Moderate
Trail surface: Paved path; considered wheel-
chair accessible
Approximate hiking time: 30 minutes
Blaze color: No blazes
County: White
Land status: National forest

Trail contact: Anna Ruby Falls Visitor Center;
(706) 878-3574; www.fs.fed.us
FYI: Park is open 9 a.m. to 7 p.m. from Memorial Day to Labor Day; 9 a.m. to 5 p.m. after
Labor Day; small day-use fee per vehicle; gift
shop, restrooms, vending machines, trash cans
at the trailhead
Maps: DeLorme: Georgia Atlas & Gazetteer:
Page 15 E9

Finding the trailhead: From the junction of GA 356 and GA 75, drive north on GA 356 for
1.25 miles. Turn left onto Anna Ruby Falls Road at the sign for USFS ANNA RUBY FALLS and travel 2.4
miles to the gate/fee booth. Pay the fee and continue another 0.9 mile to where the road dead-
ends at a large parking area.

From the junction of GA 356 and GA 197, drive south on GA 356 for 9.35 miles. Turn right
onto Anna Ruby Falls Road at the sign for USFS ANNA RUBY FALLS and follow the directions above.

GPS: N34 45.469 / W83 42.605

The Hike

The paved trail to Anna Ruby Falls is considered wheelchair accessible. Be aware,
however, that the trail to the observation deck at the base of the falls is a very steep
uphill climb. Interpretive signs along the wide path describe many of the natural fea-
tures, and benches are provided for those needing a break from the incline.

The paved path makes a steady incline, following the creek upstream until you
arrive at a footbridge. Cross the bridge and continue on the now steeper ascent until
you arrive at the observation decks at the base of Anna Ruby Falls.

The two waterfalls that make up Anna Ruby Falls sit side by side and unite to
form Smith Creek, which flows directly into Unicoi Lake.

Shortly after the Civil War, the falls and the many acres surrounding them
belonged to Col. John H. Nichols. Sadly, Colonel Nichols was a widower who had
lost not just his wife but also his two infant sons. All that was left for this decorated
war veteran was his daughter, Anna Ruby. She lives on through the splendor of Smith
and York Creeks as they create the natural wonder known as Anna Ruby Falls.

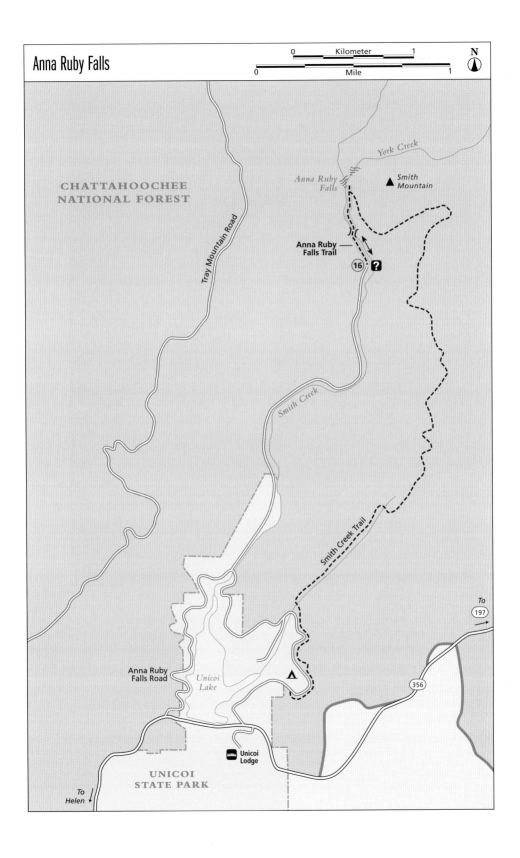

Anna Ruby Falls

York Creek

Anna Ruby
Falls

▲ Smith
Mountain

CHATTAHOOCHEE
NATIONAL FOREST

Tray Mountain Road

Anna Ruby
Falls Trail

16 ?

Smith Creek

Smith Creek Trail

To
197

Anna Ruby
Falls Road

Unicoi
Lake

356

Unicoi
Lodge

UNICOI
STATE PARK

To
Helen

Smith Creek flows to create the larger cascade of Anna Ruby Falls.

Miles and Directions

0.0   From the trailhead, hike north on the paved path. The trail makes a steep ascent as it follows the creek upstream.

0.2   Cross the creek on a footbridge and continue hiking north as the trail becomes even steeper.

0.4   Arrive at the observation decks at the base of Anna Ruby Falls (N34 45.813 / W83 42.731). Return the way you came.

0.8   Arrive back at the trailhead.

17 Flat Branch Falls

Soulful! This waterfall lies obscured from the masses. Located within the Tallulah River Basin, Flat Branch and the many other creeks found here flow freely into the grand Tallulah River.

Height: 100 feet
Beauty rating: Good
Distance: 0.5 mile out and back
Difficulty: Strenuous
Trail surface: Hard-packed dirt
Approximate hiking time: 30 minutes
Blaze color: Blue surveyor's tape tied to trees

County: Rabun
Land status: National forest
Trail contact: Chattahoochee National Forest, Chattooga Ranger District; (706) 754-6221; www.fs.fed.us
Maps: *DeLorme: Georgia Atlas & Gazetteer:* Page 16 B1

Finding the trailhead: From the junction of US 76 west and US 441 in Clayton, drive west on US 76 for 7.9 miles. Turn right onto Persimmon Road at the sign for TALLULAH RIVER CAMPGROUND and travel 4.0 miles to a left turn onto Tallulah River Road (FS 70). Continue for 1.4 miles to the Tallulah River Campground. Bypass the campground and continue straight ahead on the now unpaved Tallulah River Road for another 1.7 miles until you've crossed the fourth bridge past the Tallulah River Campground. Immediately after crossing the fourth bridge, park in the small pull-off on the right.

From the junction of US 76 and GA 197, go east on US 76 for 3.0 miles. Turn left onto Persimmon Road at the sign for TALLULAH RIVER CAMPGROUND and follow the directions above.

The trailhead is located at the south end of the bridge on the east side of the road. GPS: N34 56.770/W83 33.019

The Hike

The trail has been recently cleared and marked with blue surveyor's tape, so it should be easier followed than in days past. Follow the hidden, narrow trail as it takes you steeply uphill and into the woods. As you follow the strenuous incline, bypass what sounds like the falls on the left, and continue hiking until you reach some very large boulders on the left. Continue past the boulders on the right, following the trail until you reach the creek. Follow the creek upstream as you continue to climb toward the falls.

Trust me, you'll know when you've reached this one. Flat Branch Falls is a huge 100-foot rockslide that cannot be mistaken. Do not be deceived by the shortness of this trail. This is a very strenuous hike. If you are a hard-core waterfall hunter, it's worth the climb. Others should skip this one and head down the road another 3.3 miles to nearby Denton Branch Falls instead.

There are many theories on the origin of the word *Tallulah*. The story I enjoy most is that of a Native American village named "Ta-lu-lu," which sat along the

Flat Branch Falls and Denton Branch Falls

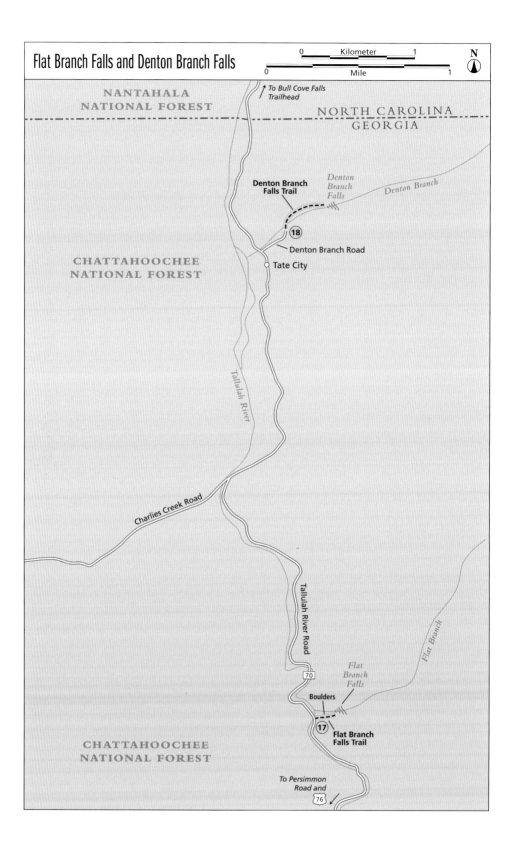

To Bull Cove Falls
Trailhead

NANTAHALA
NATIONAL FOREST

NORTH CAROLINA
GEORGIA

Denton
Branch
Falls

Denton Branch

Denton Branch
Falls Trail

18

Denton Branch Road

CHATTAHOOCHEE
NATIONAL FOREST

Tate City

Tallulah River

Charlies Creek Road

Tallulah River Road

Flat
Branch
Falls

Flat Branch

70

Boulders

17 Flat Branch
Falls Trail

CHATTAHOOCHEE
NATIONAL FOREST

To Persimmon
Road and

76

Kilometer
0   1
0   Mile   1

N

Always hike within your limits.

river's edge. The village once stood where Lake Burton sits today and was said to have gotten its name from the sounds of a certain native frog that could be heard echoing throughout the valley *ta lu lu lu lu!*

Miles and Directions

0.0   From the trailhead, hike northeast up the very steep hill and into the woods. As you follow the strenuous incline, bypass what sounds to be the falls on the left.

0.1   Reach some very large boulders on the left. Go around them on the right and continue hiking southeast.

0.2   The trail leads to the creek. Head right (northeast) here and continue climbing as you follow the creek upstream.

0.25   Arrive at Flat Branch Falls (N34 56.784 / W83 32.890). Return the way you came.

0.5   Arrive back at the trailhead.

18 Denton Branch Falls

Splendid! Denton Branch Falls is one you'll probably have to yourself—and a splendid experience it should be.

See map on page 62.
Height: 40 feet
Beauty rating: Very good
Distance: 0.6 mile out and back
Difficulty: Easy
Blaze color: No blazes
County: Rabun

Land status: National forest
Trail contact: Chattahoochee National Forest, Chattooga Ranger District; (706) 754-6221; www.fs.fed.us
Maps: *DeLorme: Georgia Atlas & Gazetteer: Page 16 A1; DeLorme: North Carolina Atlas & Gazetteer: Page 51 F6*

Finding the trailhead: From the junction of US 76 west and US 441, drive west on US 76 for 7.9 miles. Turn right onto Persimmon Road at the sign for Tallulah River Campground and travel 4.0 miles to a left turn onto Tallulah River Road (FS 70). Continue for 1.4 miles to the Tallulah River Campground. Bypass the campground and continue straight ahead on the now unpaved Tallulah River Road for another 5.0 miles. Turn right onto Denton Branch Road, an unmarked dirt road and the first right turn after Chapple Lane, a short distance past the Valley Community Church. Follow Denton Branch Road for approximately 0.2 mile to where it dead-ends at the creek.

From the junction of US 76 and GA 197, go east on US 76 for 3.0 miles. Turn left onto Persimmon Road at the sign for Tallulah River Campground and follow the directions above.

GPS: N34 59.030/W83 33.174

The Hike

The Denton Branch Trail is the continuation of Denton Branch Road. Follow the old roadbed as it heads north and cross the creek on foot. Continue upward on the old road, which soon becomes a narrow path and leads to a fork. Head right at the fork and follow the footpath toward the creek. Continue on the narrow path as you make your way uphill, following the creek upstream until the large and powerful Denton Branch Falls comes into view. The trail takes you across the creek once more to reach an island at the base of Denton Branch Falls.

Located within the Southern Nantahala Wilderness, Denton Branch, along with many other creeks, is part of the Tallulah River Basin. What that means is that they all flow into and feed the mighty Tallulah River. As you make your way to the trailhead, be sure to take a moment to appreciate the grand final product—the Tallulah River— as you pass it by. With its plentiful cascades, this river is always a pleasure.

Denton Branch is a treasure hidden in the mist.

Miles and Directions

0.0   From the trailhead, head north across the creek. Continue upward on the old roadbed as it bends right (east) and then becomes a narrow path.

0.1   Come to a fork, with an overgrown old roadbed leading up and to the left (north) and a narrow footpath leading to the right (southeast) and toward the creek. Go right (southeast) on the narrow footpath as it makes its way uphill and upstream.

0.3   Cross the creek east-southeast to reach an island at the base of Denton Branch Falls (N34 59.136 / W83 32.941). Return the way you came.

0.6   Arrive back at the trailhead.

19 Bull Cove Falls

Solitary! Almost aloof, Bull Cove Falls stands out in its stately manner above and very different from the rest of the many playful smaller cascades on the creek. Although Bull Cove Falls is located in North Carolina, you must drive into and through Tate City, Georgia, to access the trailhead. While in the area, you can also visit nearby Denton Branch Falls.

Height: 40 feet
Beauty rating: Good
Distance: 2.2 miles out and back
Difficulty: Strenuous
Trail surface: Hard-packed dirt
Approximate hiking time: 1 hour, 30 minutes
Blaze color: Blue
County: Clay

Land status: National forest
Trail contact: Nantahala National Forest, Tusquitee Ranger District; (828) 837-5152; www.fs.fed.us
Maps: *DeLorme: Georgia Atlas & Gazetteer:* Page 16 A1; *DeLorme: North Carolina Atlas & Gazetteer:* Page 51 F6

Finding the trailhead: From the junction of US 76 west and US 441, drive west on US 76 for 7.9 miles. Turn right onto Persimmon Road at the sign for Tallulah River Campground and travel 4.0 miles to a left turn onto Tallulah River Road (FS 70). Continue for 1.4 miles to the Tallulah River Campground. Bypass the campground and continue straight ahead on the now unpaved Tallulah River Road for another 5.95 miles (entering North Carolina) to a parking area on the left with a sign for the Beech Creek Trailhead.

From the junction of US 76 and GA 197, drive east on US 76 for 3.0 miles. Turn left onto Persimmon Road at the sign for Tallulah River Campground and follow the directions above.

The trailhead for Bull Cove Falls is located on the opposite (east) side of the road from where you parked and approximately 50 feet to the south. GPS: N34 59.895 / W83 33.385

The Hike

The trailhead is marked with blue blazes on the trees and a sign for Trail #378, which is the Beech Creek Trail. The dirt path heads steeply uphill and into the woods. Once in the forest, the trail traverses several switchbacks as it slowly climbs. When you finally reach the top of the hill, the trail flattens out to give you a breather before beginning a steep descent to Beech Creek.

Ford the creek and then head left, following the trail upstream to a T junction. Go left here and you soon come to rock-hop across a tributary. As the trail continues to lead upstream, you can hear the sounds of many splendid small cascades. Bypass these and continue until you reach the creek again.

Cross the creek and head right (upstream) on the very narrow, overgrown path. You will pass several smaller falls, but don't be fooled. Continue your near bushwhack as you make your way upstream to the much larger and more powerful Bull Cove Falls,

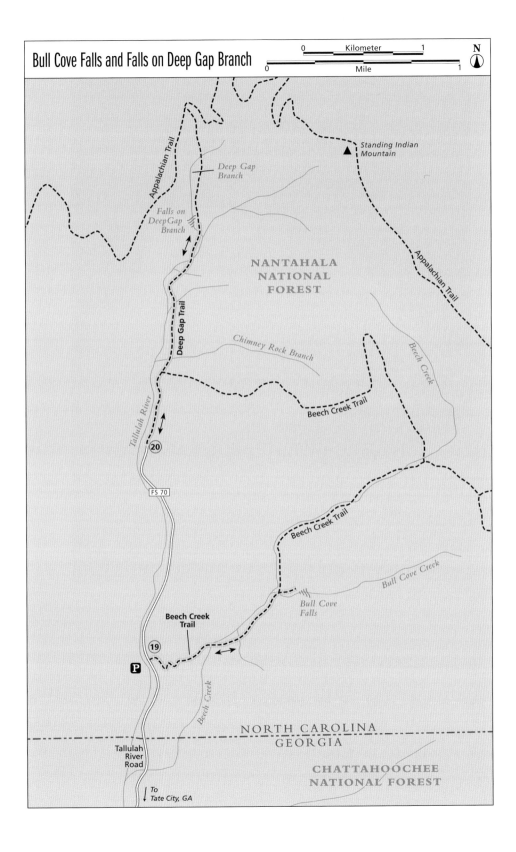

Bull Cove Falls and Falls on Deep Gap Branch

0 ─── Kilometer ─── 1

0 ─── Mile ─── 1

N

Appalachian Trail

Deep Gap
Branch

Standing Indian
Mountain

Falls on
Deep Gap
Branch

Appalachian Trail

NANTAHALA
NATIONAL
FOREST

Deep Gap Trail

Chimney Rock Branch

Beech Creek

Beech Creek Trail

Tallulah River

20

FS 70

Beech Creek Trail

Bull Cove Creek

Beech Creek
Trail

Bull Cove
Falls

19

P

Beech Creek

NORTH CAROLINA
GEORGIA

Tallulah
River
Road

CHATTAHOOCHEE
NATIONAL FOREST

To
Tate City, GA

Savor the calm before the storm on the Tallulah River.

identified by the logs that lie amidst both the lower and upper sections of the falls.

Please beware! While hiking the final portion of this trail alongside the creek, my dog, Mikey, and I were *viciously* attacked by yellow jackets from an underground nest. I highly recommend carrying Benadryl with you or, if you have known allergies, an EpiPen, just in case.

You can't help but notice Tate City as you pass through it on your way to the trailhead. What really stands out is the barn with SEE TATE CITY painted on it in bold letters and the official road sign that reads TATE CITY—POPULATION 32 +/-. This sleepy little town is said to be one of the oldest settled areas in these mountains. It was once a thriving community known for its corundum mines. When the mines dried up, the town became a lumber camp. After the lumber boom ended, Tate City eventually evolved into what you see today.

▶ **The southern yellow jacket is commonly mistaken for a bee when in fact it's a wasp. These sinister stingers often live in underground nests, and a single colony can contain as many as 100,000 yellow jackets.**

Miles and Directions

0.0 From the trailhead, follow the dirt path east as it heads steeply uphill and into the woods. Almost immediately come to a fork; go left (north) at the fork.

0.1 Come to a T junction. Go left (east) at the T; the trail continues to climb before leading to another fork. Go right (south-southeast) here. The trail slowly traverses a few switchbacks as you make your way uphill.

0.3 Reach the top of the hill; the trail bends left (northeast).

0.6 The trail leads down to Beech Creek. Ford the creek and then head left (east), following the creek upstream.

0.7 Come to a T junction and go left (east-northeast). After hiking a short distance, reach a tributary. Rock-hop across and continue hiking north-northeast.

1.0 The rocky path crosses the creek one last time. After crossing, head right (east) and follow the creek upstream on the very narrow path.

1.1 Arrive at the base of Bull Cove Falls (N35 00.184 / W83 32.561). Return the way you came.

2.2 Arrive back at the trailhead.

20 Falls on Deep Gap Branch

Challenging! With a unicorn-like tree standing out from the top of the falls, this trail is nearly as challenging as it would be to capture a real unicorn. What begins as an easy-to-follow trail ends up as a hard-core bushwhack. Although Falls on Deep Gap Branch is located in North Carolina, you must drive through Tate City, Georgia, to access the trailhead. While in the area, you can also visit nearby Denton Branch Falls.

See map on page 67.
Height: 40 feet
Beauty rating: Fair
Distance: 2.6 miles out and back
Difficulty: Strenuous
Trail surface: Hard-packed dirt
Approximate hiking time: 2 hours
Blaze color: Blue

County: Clay
Land status: National forest
Trail contact: Nantahala National Forest, Tusquitee Ranger District; (828) 837-5152; www.fs.fed.us
Maps: *DeLorme: Georgia Atlas & Gazetteer:* Page 16 A1; *DeLorme: North Carolina Atlas & Gazetteer:* Page 51 F6

Finding the trailhead: From the junction of US 76 west and US 441, drive west on US 76 for 7.9 miles. Turn right onto Persimmon Road at the sign for Tallulah River Campground and travel 4.0 miles to a left turn onto Tallulah River Road (FS 70). Continue for 1.4 miles to the Tallulah River Campground. Bypass the campground and continue straight ahead on the now unpaved Tallulah River Road for another 7.0 miles (entering North Carolina) to where the road comes to a dead end.

From the junction of US 76 and GA 197, drive east on US 76 for 3.0 miles. Turn left onto Persimmon Road at the sign for Tallulah River Campground and follow the directions above.

The trailhead is located at the north end of the parking area. GPS: N35 00.834 / W83 33.378

The Hike

The trail begins by going around the boulders and heading uphill as you enter the Southern Nantahala Wilderness. The wide roadlike trail narrows after the first 0.1 mile before crossing an open area and reaching a fork. Head left at the fork, following the Deep Gap Trail (#377). The trail leads across a creek as you continue to follow the Tallulah River upstream for another 0.3 mile. Along the way you will rock-hop a few tiny tributaries before returning to the river.

This time, instead of crossing the river, head right as you continue to follow the blue-blazed Deep Gap Trail upstream. You will cross another stream and a wet-weather tributary as the trail narrows and becomes no longer blazed. As you continue

No towel is needed at this river crossing.

the uphill trek, you rock-hop across the creek once more.

Continue steeply uphill for less than 0.25 mile more and come to the creek one last time. Do not cross it. Instead head to your left and *bushwhack* your way upstream to Falls on Deep Gap Branch. I've given this one a beauty rating of fair mainly because there isn't anywhere to perch and enjoy its full beauty.

Miles and Directions

0.0 From the trailhead, go around the boulders and up the hill to a large trail information sign for the Southern Nantahala Wilderness. Continue north past the sign on the wide roadlike trail.

0.3 The trail crosses an open area. Continue on the rocky path as it leads northwest and upward.

0.4 Come to a fork and go left (north) following the Deep Gap Trail (#377). Soon come to a creek. Cross it and continue hiking northeast as you follow the river upstream.

0.7 Arrive at the river, but do not cross. Instead head right (east), still following the trail upstream.

0.8 Come to another small stream crossing. Rock-hop across and continue northwest.

1.0 Rock-hop across yet another small, wet-weather tributary, and pick up the trail on the other side as it heads to the right (northeast). The now unblazed trail is much narrower as you trek uphill.

1.1 Come to another creek crossing. Cross it and head right (north) as you begin to climb steeply.

1.2 Reach the creek one last time, but do not cross it; instead head to the left (north) and bushwhack your way upstream toward the falls.

1.3 Arrive at the base of Falls on Deep Gap Branch (N35 01.812 / W83 33.096). Return the way you came.

2.6 Arrive back at the trailhead.

Options: If you've got some extra energy after visiting Falls on Deep Gap Branch, you could continue hiking on the Deep Gap trail for less than a mile to where it dead-ends near Deep Gap on the Appalachian Trail (AT). If you really want to spruce up the adventure, the Standing Indian Shelter sits less than a mile north on the AT. You could make this an overnight trip and stay at the shelter, but be prepared, this area tends to get quite cold at night.

While Big Laurel Falls sits geographically near Falls on Deep Gap Branch, you must drive several miles away to access it. Denton Branch Falls, however, lies right around the bend. If you've come all the way out through Tate City, Georgia, to see this one, I recommend making a day of it and visiting Denton Branch and Bull Cove Falls as well. Big Laurel and Mooney Falls could be coupled as a separate outing.

21 Hemlock Falls

Light and Lively! On the Author's Favorites List, not only the falls themselves, but the hike as well, is one experience you are sure to enjoy.

Height: 15 feet
Beauty rating: Excellent
Distance: 1.6 miles out and back
Difficulty: Easy
Trail surface: Hard-packed dirt
Approximate hiking time: 45 minutes
Blaze color: Green

County: Rabun
Land status: National forest
Trail contact: Chattahoochee National Forest, Chattooga Ranger District; (706) 754-6221; www.fs.fed.us
Maps: *DeLorme: Georgia Atlas & Gazetteer:* Page 16 C1

Finding the trailhead: From the junction of GA 197 and US 76, drive south on GA 197 for 3.6 miles. Turn right onto Andersonville Lane (immediately after passing Moccasin Creek State Park) at the sign for HEMLOCK FALLS and travel 0.4 mile to a three-way intersection. Go straight ahead at the intersection and continue another 0.1 mile to where the road dead-ends at the trailhead.

From the junction of GA 197 and GA 356, drive north on GA 197 for 7.6 miles. Turn left onto Andersonville Lane at the sign for HEMLOCK FALLS and follow the directions above.

The trailhead for Hemlock Falls Trail (#50) is identified by a very large rock with Hemlock Falls Trail etched into it. GPS: N34 50.881 / W83 35.804

The Hike

This easily followed trail makes its way back into the woods and leads past an amazing forest of ferns. As you make your way deeper into the forest, you will see several small side trails shooting off to the right. Bypass them all, staying on the wider main path. This thoroughly pleasant hike follows alongside Moccasin Creek for most of the way, giving you incredible views of the creek as it "trips and falls over stones in its way."

The creek seems alive here, and the diversity of the flora really catches your eye. Who knew there could be so many shades of green? You will pass a lovely small waterfall that flows into the creek from the opposite side before coming to a wooden footbridge atop another wonderful small waterfall.

Cross the bridge and head up the stony path. Just around the bend is the base of beautiful Hemlock Falls. You can follow the trail a short distance farther to reach the brink of Hemlock Falls, but I prefer the view from the base. The brink does not offer any fabulous mountain vistas, simply another look at the creek.

As Moccasin Creek flows peacefully into Lake Burton, it is graced with Hemlock Falls. As is typical to the area, the falls are surrounded by a hardwood forest as well as plentiful rhododendron and mountain laurel. Pine, oak, birch, and hemlock trees

This nonvenomous snake is probably more afraid of you than you are of it.

prevail. Aside from hiking, trout fishing is also a popular activity. How could it not be, with the Lake Burton Fish Hatchery as its neighbor?

Miles and Directions

0.0   From the trailhead, hike northwest back into the woods and past an amazing forest of ferns.

0.4   Look across the creek to where a small waterfall flows into the creek from above on the opposite (north) side.

WATER MOCCASINS

Commonly known as "cottonmouths," water moccasins are a venomous species of snake. They are widespread throughout the South and known for their aggressive nature. These pit vipers can be identified by their large diamond-shaped head, which has a pit on each side of it, located between the nostril and the eye. These pits are where the venom is stored. The snake's hollow fangs act like hypodermic needles, injecting venom into its prey.

If you get bitten by any snake, venomous or not, stay calm and immediately seek medical attention.

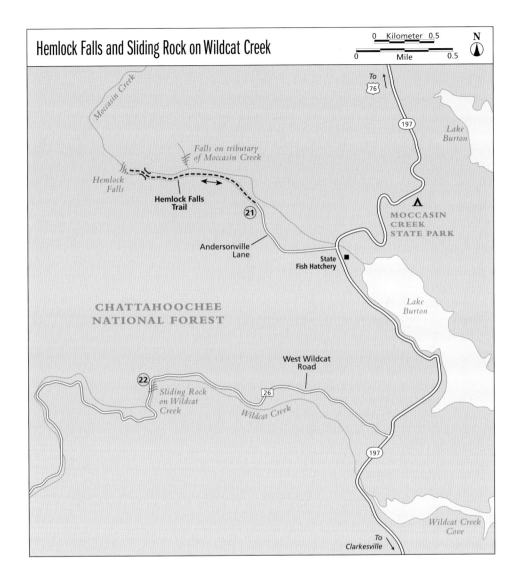

Hemlock Falls and Sliding Rock on Wildcat Creek

0   Kilometer   0.5

0   Mile   0.5

N

Moccasin Creek

To 76

197

Lake Burton

Falls on tributary of Moccasin Creek

Hemlock Falls

Hemlock Falls Trail

21

▲ MOCCASIN CREEK STATE PARK

Andersonville Lane

State Fish Hatchery ■

CHATTAHOOCHEE NATIONAL FOREST

Lake Burton

West Wildcat Road

22

Sliding Rock on Wildcat Creek

26

Wildcat Creek

197

Wildcat Creek Cove

To Clarkesville

0.7 Come to a wooden footbridge atop a wonderful small waterfall. Cross the bridge and head west up the stony path.

0.8 Arrive at Hemlock Falls (N34 51.021 / W83 36.499). Return the way you came.

1.6 Arrive back at the trailhead.

22 Sliding Rock on Wildcat Creek

Exhilarating! A favorite area waterslide and swimming hole with the local kids, the cool refreshing waters of Wildcat Creek make for a fun and exciting time. I've occasionally slid down this one myself. I once thought this one was unknown except by the locals. But when I found this Sliding Rock already exposed on the web, I decided to include it here as well.

See map on page 75.

Height: 20 feet
Beauty rating: Excellent
Distance: Roadside
Difficulty: Easy
Blaze color: No blazes
County: Rabun

Land status: National forest
Trail contact: Chattahoochee National Forest, Chattooga Ranger District; (706) 754-6221; www.fs.fed.us
Maps: *DeLorme: Georgia Atlas & Gazetteer:* Page 16 C1

Finding the trailhead: From the junction of GA 197 and US 76, drive south on GA 197 for 4.85 miles. Turn right onto West Wildcat Road (FS 26) and travel 1.5 miles to the rockslide on the left. There are several small pull-offs in the area on your left.

From the junction of GA 197 and GA 356, drive north on GA 197 for 6.3 miles. Turn left onto West Wildcat Road (FS 26) and follow the directions above; pull-offs will be on the right.

GPS: N34 50.071 / W83 36.381

The Hike

A short climb down the bank from the roadside takes you to the base of the Sliding Rock on Wildcat Creek. Special thanks go out to Brian at Burton Woods Cabins for sharing this fun and special place with us all!

Caution: There may be logs, rocks, etc., underneath the water at the base of this and all "sliding rocks." Please use caution and swim the area prior to making your initial slide.

Near Lake Burton, Wildcat Creek is located within the Lake Burton Wildlife Management Area. Besides containing this great swimming hole, the 12,600-acre WMA is well known for activities such as hunting, fishing, and hiking. Birders and those simply out for an afternoon picnic can be found here as well.

Check the creek at the base before you slide down any sliding rock, like this one on Wildcat Creek.

23 Panther and Angel Falls

Sumptuous! The trail to Panther and Angel Falls (also known as the Rabun Beach Trail) gives the hiker two waterfalls for the price of one. Fairly similar in appearance, they both resemble a staircase carved out by Mother Nature. You can't help but wonder how long it took to create such a phenomenon.

Height: Panther Falls, 50 feet; Angel Falls, 65 feet
Beauty rating: Good
Distance: Panther Falls, 1.2 miles; Angel Falls, 1.6 miles out and back
Difficulty: Panther Falls, easy to moderate; Angel Falls, moderate to strenuous
Trail surface: Hard-packed dirt
Approximate hiking time: Panther Falls, 40 minutes; Angel Falls, 1 hour, 10 minutes

Blaze color: Green
County: Rabun
Land status: National forest
Trail contact: Chattahoochee National Forest, Chattooga Ranger District; (706) 754-6221; www.fs.fed.us
FYI: Small fee to park and hike here
Maps: *DeLorme: Georgia Atlas & Gazetteer:* Page 16 D2

Finding the trailhead: From the junction of US 441 and US 76 east, drive south on US 441 for 8.9 miles. Turn right onto Old 441 south and follow it for 2.5 miles to a left turn onto Lake Rabun Road. Continue for 4.6 miles and turn right into Rabun Beach Recreation Area #2. Once inside the recreation area, immediately turn right (bypass this fee station; there is another one at the trailhead) and travel a little more than 0.1 mile to a parking area on the right, next to the phone booth.

From the junction of US 441 and the north end of the Riley C. Thurmond Bridge, drive north on US 441 for 1.7 miles. Turn left onto Old 441 south and follow the directions above.

From the junction of GA 197 and GA 356, drive north on GA 197 for 3.0 miles. Turn right onto Burton Dam Road at the Chevron Gas Station/Brooks Lil General Store and travel 8.8 miles to a left turn into the Rabun Beach Recreation Area #2 at the tiny sign for Camping Area #2. Along the way, Burton Dam Road becomes Seed Lake Road and then Lake Rabun Road. After turning into the recreation area, follow the directions above.

From the junction of GA 197 and US 76, drive south on GA 197 for 8.2 miles. Turn left onto Burton Dam Road at the Chevron Gas Station/Brooks Lil General Store and travel 8.8 miles to a left turn into the Rabun Beach Recreation Area #2 at the tiny sign for Camping Area #2. Along the way Burton Dam Road becomes Seed Lake Road and then Lake Rabun Road. After turning into the recreation area, follow the directions above.

The clearly marked trailhead for the Angel Falls Trail (#55) is located northwest of the parking area. GPS: N34 45.674/W83 28.375

Mother Nature's stair "steps" create Panther Falls.

The Hike

Follow the trail into the woods and immediately cross Joe Creek at the base of a wonderful stairwaylike waterfall. The trail then begins its incline as it follows the creek upstream. This easy-to-follow path takes you across four more footbridges before making its final, steeper ascent to the base of Panther Falls.

From the base of Panther Falls, a steep and narrow trail leads up and to the left (southwest) toward Angel Falls. Follow this trail as it climbs around a switchback and then takes you past the brink of Panther Falls. From here the trail takes you across a final wooden footbridge before reaching a fork just a short distance from Angel Falls. From the fork, you can go either way; both paths take you to the taller, narrower Angel Falls, creating a tiny loop in the trail.

With 25 miles of shoreline, beautiful Lake Rabun has been a popular recreation area since the 1930s, when the first homesites were built. A variety of activities can be enjoyed here in addition to hiking, including fishing, boating, swimming, picnicking, and camping.

BIG CATS

Oddly enough, the genus *Panthera* does not classify what is typically referred to as a panther. The big cats with the *Panthera* classification are jaguars, lions, tigers, and leopards. These colorful cats are the only ones that can roar. The mountain lion (*Felis concolor*), which is commonly referred to as cougar, puma, and regionally as panther, belongs to the genus *Felis*. Identified by their solid-colored coats, many of these big cats are threatened or endangered. These feral felines are said to be extinct in the Southern Appalachians, although several sightings have been reported. So if you're fortunate enough to spot one in the wild—or even think you do, be sure to shoot it only with the lens of your camera.

Miles and Directions

0.0 From the trailhead, hike north into the woods. Immediately cross the creek at the base of a wonderful stairwaylike waterfall. From here the trail begins its incline as it follows Joe Creek upstream.

0.3 Cross a footbridge and continue hiking north.

0.4 Cross another footbridge; continue hiking northwest.

0.5 Cross a third and fourth footbridge and continue hiking northwest as the trail begins its steeper ascent.

0.6 Arrive at the base of Panther Falls (N34 46.070 / W83 28.633). From the base of Panther Falls, a narrow trail heads steeply uphill to the left (southwest). Follow this trail as it climbs around a switchback and leads to the brink of Panther Falls.

0.7 The easily followed trail takes you across one final footbridge. Continue hiking north-northeast.

0.8 Come to a fork in the trail. Go either way here; these two trails make a tiny loop, and both lead to Angel Falls (N34 46.268 / W83 28.695). Return the way you came.

1.6 Arrive back at the trailhead.

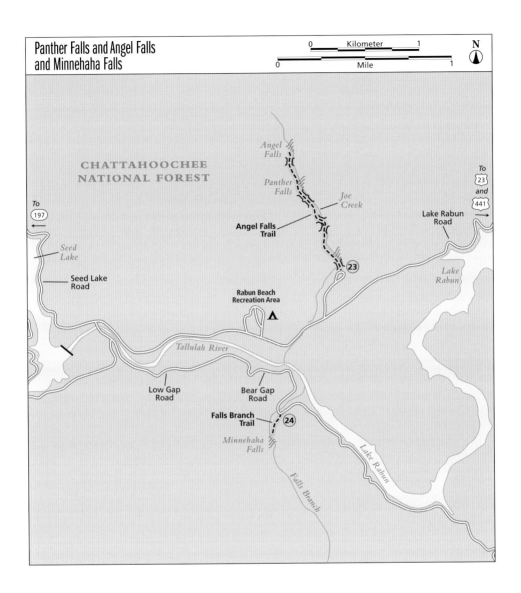

Panther Falls and Angel Falls
and Minnehaha Falls

0   Kilometer   1

0   Mile   1

N

CHATTAHOOCHEE
NATIONAL FOREST

Angel
Falls

Panther
Falls

Joe
Creek

To
23
and
441

Angel Falls
Trail

Lake Rabun
Road

To
197

Seed
Lake

Lake
Rabun

Seed Lake
Road

Rabun Beach
Recreation Area

Tallulah River

Low Gap
Road

Bear Gap
Road

Falls Branch
Trail

24

Minnehaha
Falls

Lake Rabun

Falls Branch

24 Minnehaha Falls

Terrific! The trail to Minnehaha Falls is also known as the Falls Branch Trail. Surprisingly, this waterfall does not seem to get a lot of traffic or praise. To me, however, Minnehaha seems almost alive. Teeming with character and uplifting in spirit, I highly recommend the "laughing waters" of Minnehaha.

See map on page 81.
Height: 55 feet
Beauty rating: Excellent
Distance: 0.4 mile out and back
Difficulty: Easy to moderate
Trail surface: Hard-packed dirt
Approximate hiking time: 15 minutes
Blaze color: No blazes

County: Rabun
Land status: National forest
Trail contact: Chattahoochee National Forest, Chattooga Ranger District; (706) 754-6221; www.fs.fed.us
Maps: *DeLorme: Georgia Atlas & Gazetteer:* Page 16 D2

Finding the trailhead: From the junction of US 441 and US 76 east, drive south on US 441 for 8.9 miles. Turn right onto Old 441 south and travel 2.5 miles to a left turn onto Lake Rabun Road. Continue 6.2 miles before turning left onto Low Gap Road (where Lake Rabun Road becomes Seed Lake Road). Immediately turn left and drive over the bridge across Seed Lake. After approximately 0.1 mile, Low Gap Road makes a sharp bend to the right and a dirt road continues straight ahead. This dirt road is Bear Gap Road. Follow it along the lakeside for 1.5 miles to a small pull-off on the left.

From the junction of US 441 and the north end of the Riley C. Thurmond Bridge, drive north on US 441 for 1.7 miles. Turn left onto Old 441 south and follow the directions above.

From the junction of GA 197 and SR 356, drive north on GA 197 for 3.0 miles. Turn right onto Burton Dam Road at the Chevron Gas Station/Brooks Lil General Store and travel 7.2 miles. Turn right onto Low Gap Road (along the way, Burton Dam Road becomes Seed Lake Road) and follow the directions above.

From the junction of GA 197 and US 76, drive south on GA 197 for 8.2 miles. Turn left onto Burton Dam Road at the Chevron Gas Station/Brooks Lil General Store and continue 7.2 miles. Turn right onto Low Gap Road (along the way Burton Dam Road becomes Seed Lake Road) and follow the directions above.

GPS: N34 44.977 / W83 28.751

The Hike

Reach Minnehaha Falls by hiking on the Falls Branch Trail (#147). The trail begins by heading up some primitive steps and then continues its short but steady climb before leveling off and leading to the creek. Once at the creek, head left (south) and soon arrive at the base of Minnehaha Falls. The freshness of the cool breeze at the base of this one is truly exhilarating!

Enjoy the "curling water" at Minnehaha Falls

Minnehaha is a fictional Native American woman who was the lover of the main character in Henry Wadsworth Longfellow's poem "The Song of Hiawatha."

Hiawatha, founder of the Iroquois confederacy, and the fictional Minnehaha have lent their names to several places throughout Minnesota, including Minnehaha and Hiawatha Avenues in the city of Minneapolis. Often incorrectly translated as "laughing water," the true meaning of *Minnehaha* is "curling water" or "waterfall."

Miles and Directions

0.0 From the trailhead, head up the primitive steps and hike southwest as the trail begins a slow but steady climb.

0.2 The trail levels off and leads to the creek. Head left (south) and soon arrive at the base of Minnehaha Falls (N34 44.845 / W83 28.832). Return the way you came.

0.4 Arrive back at the trailhead.

25 Panther Creek Falls

Grandeur! Like a Phoenix in flight, this waterfall inspires and amazes all who visit. Easily making the author's favorites list, Panther Creek Falls is one of the most beautiful waterfalls in the area. A wonderful place for a picnic or a quick dip, it gets quite a few hikers, especially on the weekends. You are not likely to have this one to yourself for long, if at all.

Height: 75 feet
Beauty rating: Excellent
Distance: 7.0 miles out and back
Difficulty: Moderate
Trail surface: Hard-packed dirt
Approximate hiking time: 3 hours, 15 minutes
Blaze color: Green
County: Habersham

Land status: National forest
Trail contact: Chattahoochee National Forest, Chattooga Ranger District; (706) 754-6221; www.fs.fed.us
FYI: Open 7 a.m. to 10 p.m.; small day-use fee
Maps: *DeLorme: Georgia Atlas & Gazetteer:* Page 16 E2

Finding the trailhead: From the junction of US 441 and US 76 east, drive south on US 441 for 13.1 miles. Turn right onto Old Historic 441 (look for the sign for Panther Creek Picnic Area and Trail) and travel 1.5 miles to a right turn into the parking area for the Chattahoochee National Forest Panther Creek Area.

From the junction of US 441 and GA 17 Alternate, drive north on US 441 for 3.0 miles. Turn left onto Glenn Hardman Road just south of mile marker 18 and travel 0.1 mile to where the road dead-ends at a stop sign (a U.S. post office will be right in front of you). Go right here, continuing 1.0 mile to a left turn into the parking area for the Chattahoochee National Forest Panther Creek Area.

From the junction of GA 197 and US 76, drive south on GA 197 for 7.1 miles. Turn left onto Raper Mountain Road just before the Batesville Junction Gas Station and travel 1.8 miles to a stop sign at Oakey Mountain Road. Go left onto Oakey Mountain Road (which becomes New Liberty Road) and follow it for 7.3 miles. Turn left onto Orchard Road and continue for 5.1 miles to where it dead-ends at Old Historic Highway 441. Go left here and travel 0.6 mile before turning left into the parking area for Panther Creek Falls, just before the Chattahoochee National Forest sign for Panther Creek Area.

From the junction of GA 197 and GA 356, drive north on GA 197 for 0.8 mile. Turn right onto Raper Mountain Road just past the Batesville Junction Gas Station and follow the directions above.

The trailhead to Panther Creek Falls is located just across the street (southeast) from the parking area. GPS: N34 41.931 / W83 25.170

The Hike

The narrow trail takes you under US 441 and into an open grassy field. After crossing the field, it heads back into the woods and downhill. The trail bends left at the creek and then takes you through one more open area as you pass under some power

Everything about Panther Creek Falls is breathtaking.

lines. Don't be discouraged, the trail heads back into the forest, where it stays for the remainder of the hike.

Continue following the green blazes on the easy-to-follow trail until you reach some large boulders hanging over the trail. Continue under and around them; the well-maintained path returns once you reach the other side. Follow the trail as it twists and turns high above the creek's edge.

When you finally reach the creek at a primitive campsite, you will come to a wooden footbridge. Cross it and continue hiking downstream to another wooden footbridge. Cross this as well as you continue hiking deeper into the forest. Cross a third wooden footbridge and continue following the main trail in a generally southerly direction.

The trail now rises high above the bank of Panther Creek. After rock-hopping a small stream, the trail makes an uphill climb. You will cross a fourth footbridge, and again the trail climbs to the cliffs overhanging the creek. Guy wires act as a makeshift "guardrail" to prevent you from falling, but I don't think I'd put my full body weight on them.

The trail flattens out a bit, and you rock-hop another tributary. Again you come to a rise above the creek with guy wires. After descending this rise, stay on the main trail and continue following the creek downstream. You soon come to your third rise with guy wires. Upon coming down from this one, you find yourself out on some boulders just above the brink of Panther Creek Falls. Enjoy the view from here before

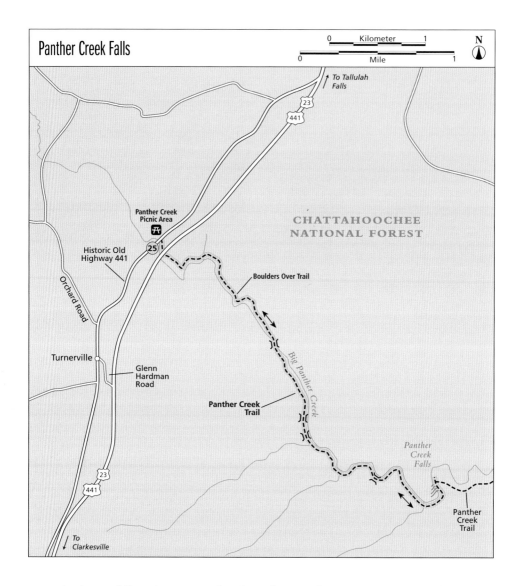

Panther Creek Falls

0 ——— Kilometer ——— 1

0 ——— Mile ——— 1

N

To Tallulah Falls

23

441

Panther Creek Picnic Area

CHATTAHOOCHEE NATIONAL FOREST

Historic Old Highway 441

25

Boulders Over Trail

Orchard Road

Turnerville

Glenn Hardman Road

Panther Creek Trail

Big Panther Creek

Panther Creek Falls

23

441

Panther Creek Trail

To Clarkesville

continuing to follow the steep path a short distance downstream over your final guy wire rise and down to the base of Panther Creek Falls.

With a sandy beach at the base and perfect panoramic views, Panther Creek Falls is a very welcome sight.

The USDA Forest Service has designated nearly 600 acres in two separate tracts along the river as the Panther Creek Botanical Area. Both tracts are located downstream from the falls and are protected due to the richness and diversity of the plant life they contain—flora that is typically uncommon in northern Georgia. The river here lies directly

▶ **Botany is one of the oldest branches of biology. Simply put, it's the study of plant life.**

on the Brevard Fault, giving the soil below an excessive amount of limestone content. It is this high concentration of limestone that allows the area to support such rare vegetation.

Miles and Directions

0.0 From the parking area, walk south back up to Old 441, cross the road, and head left (east) a very short distance to the trailhead. The narrow trail leads south and takes you under US 441 before taking you across an open grassy field.

0.5 The trail brings you through another open area, and you pass under some power lines. Continue hiking southeast and the trail leads back into the forest, where it remains for the rest of the hike.

0.8 Come to some large boulders hanging over the trail. Go south-southeast as you make your way under and around the boulders.

1.4 Reach the creek at a primitive campsite followed by a wooden footbridge. Cross the footbridge and continue hiking downstream (west-southwest).

1.9 Cross a second footbridge and continue hiking south as you make your way deeper into the forest.

2.0 Cross a third footbridge and continue to follow the Panther Creek Trail generally south. The trail now rises high above the bank of the creek.

2.3 Rock-hop a small stream. The trail makes an uphill climb as it leads southeast.

2.6 Cross a fourth footbridge. The trail again climbs to the cliffs overhanging the creek as you continue to hike southeast.

3.0 The trail flattens out a bit, and you rock-hop across another tributary. Continue east and again come to a rise above the creek, with guy wires acting as a makeshift guardrail.

3.3 Come to a third rise with guy wires. Coming down from this one, find yourself out on some boulders just above the brink of the falls. Enjoy the view from here before continuing northeast, following the trail steeply downhill.

3.5 Arrive at the sandy beach at the base of Panther Creek Falls (N34 40.638 / W83 23.288). Return the way you came.

7.0 Arrive back at the trailhead.

The lovely bearded iris is common in the Georgia mountains.

26 Waterfalls of Tallulah Gorge

Breathtaking! Tallulah Gorge offers some of the most incredible views in the area. Seven breathtaking waterfalls can be viewed here, five of which are easily visible from the rim of the gorge. Three trails will be described. First up are the North and South Rim Trails, which afford views of Oceana Falls, L'Eaud'Or Falls, Tallulah Gorge Dam, Tempesta Falls, Hurricane Falls, and Caledonia Cascade. These falls are visible from various numbered overlooks along the rim. The Gorge Floor Trail takes you down into the gorge and offers views of Bridal Veil Falls (aka Sliding Rock), Oceana Falls, and Hurricane Falls, all from the base.

Height: 46 to 96 feet
Beauty rating: Excellent
Distance: 5.0 miles out and back
Difficulty: North and South Rim Trails, easy to moderate; Gorge Floor Trail, strenuous
Trail surface: Rubber mulch path; bouldering along the river's edge
Approximate hiking time: 2 hours to hike the rim trails; up to an entire day exploring the gorge floor

Blaze color: White
County: Rabun and Habersham
Land status: State park
Trail contact: Tallulah Gorge State Park; (706) 754-7970; www.gastateparks.org
FYI: Day-use fee; Gorge Floor Trail recommended for experienced hikers only, requires permit
Maps: *DeLorme: Georgia Atlas & Gazetteer:* Page 16 E3

Finding the trailhead: From the junction of US 441 and US 76 east, drive south on US 441 for 10.4 miles. Turn left onto Jane Hurt Yarn Road at the sign for the INTERPRETIVE CENTER and travel 0.4 mile to a fork in the road with stone pillars at the entrance to the right fork. Go right here and come to a guard gate. Stop and pay the day-use fee and then continue down the hill until the road dead-ends at the visitor/interpretive center.

From the junction of US 441 and Alternate GA 17, drive north on US 441 for 7.9 miles. Turn right onto Jane Hurt Yarn Road at the sign for the INTERPRETIVE CENTER and follow the directions above.

GPS: N34 44.389 / W83 23.445

The Hikes

North Rim Trail

The North Rim Trail begins behind the Tallulah Gorge Interpretive Center and quickly leads you to a T junction. If you go left here, the trail leads past the original Wallenda tower, from which a tightrope was stretched across the gorge. After passing the tower, the trail leads to Overlook #1 and then onto the park's newest overlook, Inspiration Point. Stupendous views of the gorge can be seen in both directions from this location.

Overlook #2 provides a great view of L'Eaud'Or Falls.

After enjoying the views, backtrack to the T and head in the other direction (west) on the North Rim Trail, which leads to Overlooks # 3 and #2. Fantastic views of L'Eaud'Or Falls can be seen from both. From Overlook #2 an access point leads you down into the gorge to a suspension bridge over the Tallulah River.

Options: You could cross the suspension bridge and head up the 347 steps that lead to the South Rim Trail between Overlooks #7 and #8; you could continue down the 221 steps that take you deeper into the gorge to a platform at the base of Hurricane Falls; or you could head back the way you came and climb up the 310 steps that lead back to Overlook #2.

Tallulah Gorge Dam is impressive when seen from Overlook #4.

To continue on the recommended route, the North Rim Trail leads to Overlook #4, which affords a good view of the water falling from the Tallulah Gorge Dam. You soon arrive at Overlook #5, which gives you a nice downstream view of the gorge itself. From Overlook #5 the now paved path leads toward the bridge over the dam. Just before walking under the bridge, you will see a short set of stairs on the right that leads up to US 441. Climb up these steps and then cross the bridge above the dam, staying on the east side of US 441.

After crossing the bridge, you will see a paved path on the left heading southeast back into the woods. (**Options:** Hiking the North Rim Trail from the Visitor Center

View Hurricane Falls from the base.

to Inspiration Point and back west to Overlook 4 at the dam, then returning to the start is 1.8 miles.) Follow this path as you now begin hiking on the South Rim Trail.

South Rim Trail

Once on the South Rim Trail, follow the paved path a short distance and soon arrive at Overlook #6. Overlook #6 offers phenomenal views of Hawthorne Pool, the blue-green pool that sits at the base of L'Eaud'Or Falls. Continue along the path until you come to Overlook #7, the best place to get a good view of wondrous Tempesta Falls.

As you make your way from Overlook #7 to Overlook #8, you pass the south rim access point to the gorge. The many steps lead down to the suspension bridge and then farther down to the gorge floor, to a platform at the base of Hurricane Falls. For now, bypass these steps and continue along the South Rim Trail to Overlook #8. This is the best place to view Hurricane Falls from the rim trails.

From Overlook #8 the trail leads to a fork. Take either path—they both quickly lead to Overlook #9. The trail then continues to Overlook #10, where it dead-ends. Overlook #10 gives you a very nice view of the gorge itself, but the only waterfall you can see from here is the Caledonia Cascade as it flows 600 feet from the north rim of the gorge down into the gorge floor.

After you have hiked the two rim trails, backtrack and enter the gorge from either the south or north rim. (**Option:** Backtrack on the South and North Rim Trails to the trailhead for an out and back hike of 3.4 miles.)

Waterfalls of Tallulah Gorge

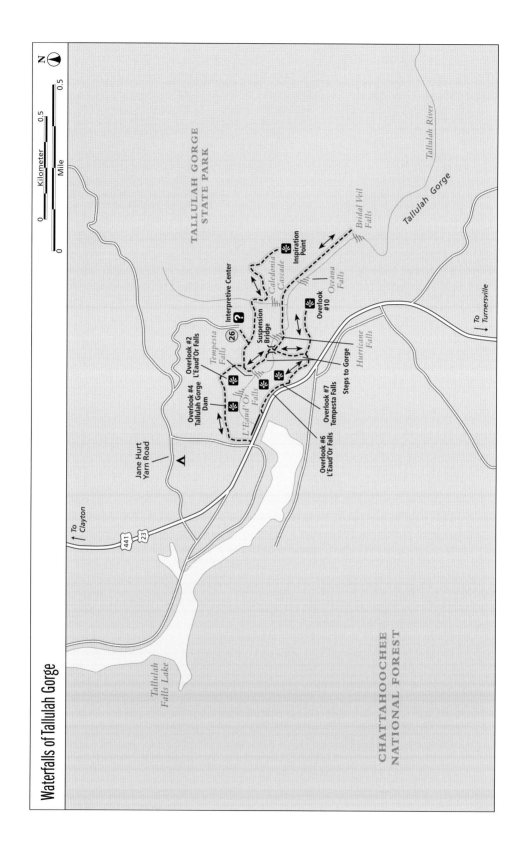

N

0   Kilometer   0.5

0   Mile   0.5

To Clayton

441
23

Tallulah Falls Lake

Jane Hurt Yarn Road

Overlook #4
Tallulah Gorge Dam

Overlook #2
L'Eaud'Or Falls

Tempesta Falls

Interpretive Center

26

L'Eaud'Or Falls

Overlook #6
L'Eaud'Or Falls

Overlook #7
Tempesta Falls

Suspension Bridge

Steps to Gorge

Caledonia Cascade

Inspiration Point

Overlook #10

Oceana Falls

Bridal Veil Falls

Hurricane Falls

TALLULAH GORGE
STATE PARK

Tallulah Gorge

Tallulah River

To Turnersville

CHATTAHOOCHEE
NATIONAL FOREST

Gorge Floor Trail

Prior to hiking the Gorge Floor Trail, you must obtain a permit from the interpretive center. Permits are free of charge but are limited to one hundred per day, so be sure to arrive early. The gorge floor permit allows you to explore the gorge from Hurricane Falls all the way downstream to Bridal Veil Falls. Fantastic views of Hurricane, Oceana, and Bridal Veil Falls can be seen from here, but be aware that there is no set trail. You have to blaze your own way downstream along the boulder-strewn river.

To enter the gorge, take the many steps that lead steeply down from either rim trail to the base of Hurricane Falls. After basking in nature's splendor here, *carefully* rock-hop across the river. I cannot stress the need for caution here enough! People have drowned while crossing the river and getting caught in the swift currents.

Once you reach the other side of the river, head up to the tree line and begin your trek downstream. Along the way you will pass the mild flow of Caledonia Cascade before reaching the brink of Oceana Falls. The downstream views of the gorge and the river are breathtaking!

From the brink continue a short distance farther to the base of Oceana Falls. After enjoying this beauty, continue to blaze your own trail downstream for another 0.5 mile and finally arrive at Bridal Veil Falls. This is the only place in the gorge where you are permitted to swim. And, yes, you are also allowed to slide down the "Sliding Rock," which is an alias for Bridal Veil Falls. Take the plunge at your own risk. Exploring the gorge floor can be dangerous. I recommend this for *experienced hikers* only!

At nearly 1,000 feet deep and 2 miles long, Tallulah Gorge creates an amazing, picturesque setting. The dam, built in 1913, changed the river's flow forever. Several times a year, however, the Georgia Power Company (which owns the dam) performs "aesthetic" water releases and whitewater releases for kayakers. They open the dam and allow you to get a peek at what the river once was in all its splendor. These water releases are performed annually on the first two weekends in April and the first three weekends in November.

As mentioned earlier, you pass right by the remains of the Wallenda tower on your way to Overlook #1. This tower once stood tall above the gorge and was used in 1970 by Karl Wallenda, who successfully walked a tightrope (with no net!) across the windy Tallulah Gorge from Overlook #1 on the north rim to another tower on the south rim. Sixteen years later, Professor Leon performed the same feat traveling in the opposite direction.

Miles and Directions

0.0 The trail leads west-northwest from the interpretive center and immediately takes you to a T junction. Going left here takes you east-southeast to Overlook #1 and then onto Inspiration Point. Going right takes you west toward Overlooks #2 and #3. Go left for now, hiking east-southeast toward Overlook #1.

0.2 Arrive at Overlook #1 (N34 44.322/W83 23.318). From Overlook #1, Oceana Falls can be viewed just downstream on the gorge floor. After enjoying the view, continue hiking east-southeast as the trail slowly climbs. (*Option:* For an easier hike, skip the moderate hike to Inspiration Point and return to the T the way you came. Once at the T, continue hiking westward on the North Rim Trail.)

0.5 Arrive at Inspiration Point (N34 44.284/W83 23.170). From here you get spectacular views of the gorge itself and can also see Oceana Falls and L'Eaud'Or Falls. Turn around and retrace your steps.

1.0 Arrive back at the T junction near the interpretive center. This time, head the other way (west) to Overlooks #2 and #3. First come to Overlook #3 (N34 44.395/W83 23.547). This overlook gives you good views of L'Eaud'Or Falls. From Overlook #3, head south toward Overlook #2.

1.1 Arrive at Overlook #2 (N34 44.368/W83 23.552). In my opinion, this is the best place on the north rim to view L'Eaud'Or Falls. From Overlook #2 backtrack and pass Overlook #3 as you make your way northwest toward Overlook #4. (*Option:* Head down the 310 steps into the gorge and cross the suspension bridge. Once on the other side, you can either head down another 221 steps to view Hurricane Falls from the base, or climb up 347 steps to come out on the South Rim Trail between Overlooks #7 and #8.)

1.4 Arrive at Overlook #4 (N34 44.433/W83 23.673), affording a view of the Tallulah Gorge Dam. After appreciating its might, continue hiking counterclockwise around the curve toward Overlook #5.

1.5 Arrive at Overlook #5 (N34 44.426/W83 23.729). This one gives you views of the gorge from the west end. After enjoying the views, follow the trail northwest and you soon see some steps on the right (west) at the sign for Sᴏᴜᴛʜ Rɪᴍ Tʀᴀɪʟ. These steps lead up to US 441. Climb the steps and then follow US 441 east-southeast over the bridge to access the South Rim Trail. (*Option:* To shorten the hike to 2.0 miles, backtrack, and return to the interpretive center.)

1.7 After crossing the bridge, go left (southeast) and begin hiking on the South Rim Trail.

1.8 Arrive at Overlook #6 (N34 44.310/W83 23.601), which provides amazing views of Hawthorne Pool. Sitting at the base of L'Eaud'Or Falls, this blue-green pool appears inviting, but the river's swift currents would be overwhelming. From Overlook #6, make your way south toward Overlook #7.

1.9 Arrive at Overlook #7 (N34 44.267/W83 23.570). Tempesta Falls can be viewed from here along with fabulous views of the gorge itself. Continue south-southeast along the south rim of the gorge.

2.0 Bypass the steps that lead into the gorge and down to a platform at the base of Hurricane Falls, For now, continue hiking east toward Overlook #8. (*Option:* Head steeply down the many steps that lead into the gorge. Amazing views of Hurricane Falls can be had from the platform at the base, but the steps make it a strenuous task.)

2.1 Arrive at Overlook #8 (N34 44.224/W83 23.417). This is the best place to view Hurricane Falls from the rim. From Overlook #8 continue hiking east and soon come to a fork. Either path quickly leads to Overlook #9 (N34 44.229/W83 23.366). This overlook gives you slight views of Hurricane Falls upstream and a fairly decent view of Oceana Falls downstream. Continue hiking southeast toward Overlook #10.

2.2 Arrive at Overlook #10 (N34 44.218/W83 23.352). While Overlook #10 does not give you views of any waterfalls, it does afford fantastic views of the gorge itself. After

A visitor from Oregon takes the plunge and slides down Bridal Veil Falls.

appreciating the view, backtrack to the steps between Overlooks #7 and #8 that head down into the gorge to the base of Hurricane Falls.

2.3 Arrive back at the steps that head down into the gorge. From here, head north, steeply down the many steps that lead into the Tallulah Gorge. (*Option:* Bypass the steps and backtrack, returning to the trailhead via the South and North Rim Trails for a hike of 3.4 miles.).

2.5 After descending 347 steps, you arrive at the suspension bridge that crosses over the gorge and acts as a shortcut back to the North Rim Trail. Bypass this for now, and continue descending another 221 steps as you make your way to the gorge floor. (*Option:* Cross the suspension bridge and head up the 310 steps that lead up to the North Rim Trail near Overlook #2.)

2.6 Reach the platform at the base of Hurricane Falls (N34 44.289 / W83 23.427). You can really feel the force of the water at the base of this one. (*Note:* You cannot step off this platform without first having obtained a permit from the interpretive center.) After enjoying the exhilarating power unleashed by Hurricane Falls, either head back out of the gorge or, if you have a permit, *carefully* rock-hop across the river. Once on the other side, scramble up to the tree line and then follow it east as you make your way downstream alongside the boulder-strewn river. (*Option:* From the platform at the base of Hurricane Falls, skip the Gorge Floor Trail and head back up the steps and out of the gorge to either the North or South Rim Trail. This would make the hike 3.0 or 3.8 miles respectively.)

2.9 Pass Caledonia Cascade (N34 44.291 / W83 23.337) as it flows down 600 feet from the north rim of the gorge. Continue to follow the river downstream (east) as you make your way farther into the Tallulah Gorge.

3.1 Arrive at the base of Oceana Falls (N34 44.249 / W83 23.254). You can't even fathom the beauty of this waterfall from the rim trails. After spending some time here, continue blazing your own trail generally south on the gorge floor as you follow the river downstream.

3.6 Arrive at Bridal Veil Falls (N34 44.091 / W83 23.086). This one is also known as Sliding Rock, and for a good reason. This is the one place in the gorge where it is deemed "safe" to swim, but do so at your own risk. You are in for a thrill and a chill here. You can actually slide down the face of Bridal Veil Falls and take the chilling plunge into the Tallulah River at the base. After cooling down in the river, the rocky faces of the river's edge make a great place to warm back up in the rays of the sun. Once you've gotten the most out of Bridal Veil Falls, backtrack upstream to the river crossing, and then make your way back up the steps to the suspension bridge across the gorge.

4.7 Arrive back at the suspension bridge (N34 44.302 / W83 23.481). Cross the suspension bridge and then head up the 310 steps that lead to the north rim near Overlook #2. (*Option:* You can return up the steps to the south rim and backtrack to the trailhead, adding 1.1 miles to the hike for a total of 6.1 miles.)

4.9 The steps bring you out of the gorge and put you onto the North Rim Trail near Overlook #2. From Overlook #2 make your way toward Overlook #3 and then head right (southeast) back toward the interpretive center.

5.0 Arrive back at the trailhead behind the interpretive center.

Options: For an easy hike, hike the North Rim Trail only, but skip the section from Overlook #1 to Inspiration Point (1.0 mile). Easy to moderate: Hike the complete North Rim Trail (2.0 miles) or hike the complete North and South Rim Trails (3.4 miles). Moderate to strenuous: Hike down into the gorge to the platform at the base of Hurricane Falls (3.0 miles if you return via the North Rim stairs, or 3.8 miles if you return via the South Rim steps). Strenuous: Hike both the North and South Rim Trails and also the Gorge Floor Trail (5.0 miles).

27 Toccoa Falls

Lavish! Toccoa Falls is absolutely delightful. One of the few waterfalls that make a true freefall, its beauty is indescribable. Despite the lack of privacy here, this highly recommended waterfall makes the Author's Favorites List.

Height: 186 feet
Beauty rating: Excellent
Distance: 0.2 mile out and back
Difficulty: Easy
Trail surface: Wide gravel trail
Approximate hiking time: 15 minutes
Blaze color: No blazes
County: Stephens

Land status: Private property
Trail contact: Toccoa Falls College; (706) 886-7299, ext. 5257; www.tfc.edu
FYI: Waterfall access is from 9 a.m. to sundown year-round; nominal fee to visit the falls
Maps: DeLorme: Georgia Atlas & Gazetteer: Page 16 F3-G3

Finding the trailhead: From the junction of US 441 and US 76 east, drive south on US 441 for 18.4 miles. Turn left onto Alternate GA 17 (GA 17A) and drive south for 8.3 miles to the entrance to Toccoa Falls College on the right at the large stone sign for Toccoa Falls College. Go through the gate and come to a stop sign. Go straight ahead, following the signs for Toccoa Falls and Gift Shop. After traveling for 0.8 mile from GA 17A, arrive at the parking area for the falls and the gift shop.

From the junction of US 441 and GA 17, drive north on US 441 for 3.6 miles. Turn right onto GA 17A and follow the directions above, turning left at the sign for Toccoa Falls College.

GPS: N34 35.645/W83 21.643

The Hike

Located on the campus of Toccoa Falls College, the falls are accessed through the gift shop. Toccoa Falls is suitable for all ages; both young and old will enjoy this one. If the gift shop is closed, the gate next to it should be open. The wide gravel trail follows the creek upstream before reaching the base of Toccoa Falls.

Toccoah means "beautiful" in Cherokee, which makes this waterfall aptly named indeed. However beautiful it may be, this was once the site of a horrible tragedy. In 1977 a dam above the falls broke, causing a flood so great that it killed thirty-nine unsuspecting people, injured more than sixty others, and caused millions of dollars in damage. With the help of local, state, and federal agencies, the college was able to rebuild and remain open. Yet the loss of

Now that's a sunrise worth waking up early for.

Toccoa Falls

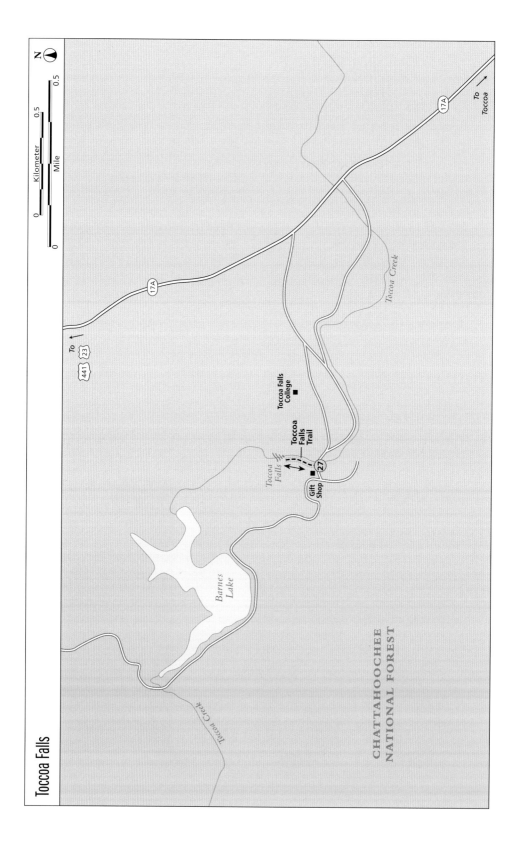

- CHATTAHOOCHEE NATIONAL FOREST
- Barnes Lake
- Toccoa Creek
- Toccoa Falls
- Toccoa Falls Trail
- Toccoa Falls College
- Gift Shop
- 27
- 17A
- To Toccoa
- To 441 23
- Toccoa Creek

N

Kilometer
0   0.5   0.5
Mile
0   0.5

The tall free-falling waters of Toccoa Falls

life that day will never be forgotten. A memorial now stands near the base of the falls to honor those souls who did not survive.

Miles and Directions

0.0 Begin by entering into the gift shop and paying a nominal fee. As you exit the gift shop, the trail follows the creek northwest and upstream.

0.1 Arrive at the base of Toccoa Falls. (N34 35.734 / W83 21.616). Return the way you came.

0.2 Arrive back at the trailhead.

28 Stonewall Falls

Reflection! Stonewall Falls is loaded with perfect ledges for sitting and reflecting on the natural beauty that surrounds you. The softly spilling water encourages thoughts of peace, harmony, and wonder.

Height: 25 feet
Beauty rating: Very good
Distance: Roadside
Difficulty: Easy
Other trail users: Mountain bikers
Blaze color: No blazes
County: Rabun

Land status: National forest
Trail contact: Chattahoochee National Forest, Chattooga Ranger District; (706) 754-6221; www.fs.fed.us
Maps: *DeLorme: Georgia Atlas & Gazetteer:* Page 16 C2

Finding the trailhead: From the junction of US 76 west and US 441, drive west on US 76 for 0.2 mile. Turn left onto Main Street and travel 3.2 miles to a four-way stop sign with a flashing red light. Continue straight ahead through the stop sign for another 2.25 miles and turn right onto FS 20 at the sign for Stonewall Falls Mountain Bike Trail. (Along the way, Main Street becomes Old Highway 441.) Continue for 1.7 miles to where the road dead-ends at a primitive campsite next to the creek. (***Note:*** At 1.2 miles on FS 20 you will pass a designated parking area with a small day-use fee. FS 20 can be a rough and bumpy ride. If you do not have a high-clearance vehicle, I advise you to park here and walk the extra 0.5 mile down FS 20 to see the falls.)

From the junction of US 76 and GA 197, drive east on US 76 for 10.7 miles. Turn right onto Main Street and follow the directions above.

GPS: N34 49.234 / W83 27.003

The Hike

Stonewall Falls sits northwest from where you parked and is visible from the creek's edge. Just look upstream to view it from the base.

You might think the falls is named for the stone wall that makes up a portion of the waterfall—a ledge so perfect you can even sit upon it. It's more likely, however, that the waterfall was named for Gen. Thomas Jonathan "Stonewall" Jackson. Jackson was a confederate general during

More than fifty species of sunflowers (genus Helianthus) are native to North America; some can grow as tall as 9 feet.

Stonewall Falls

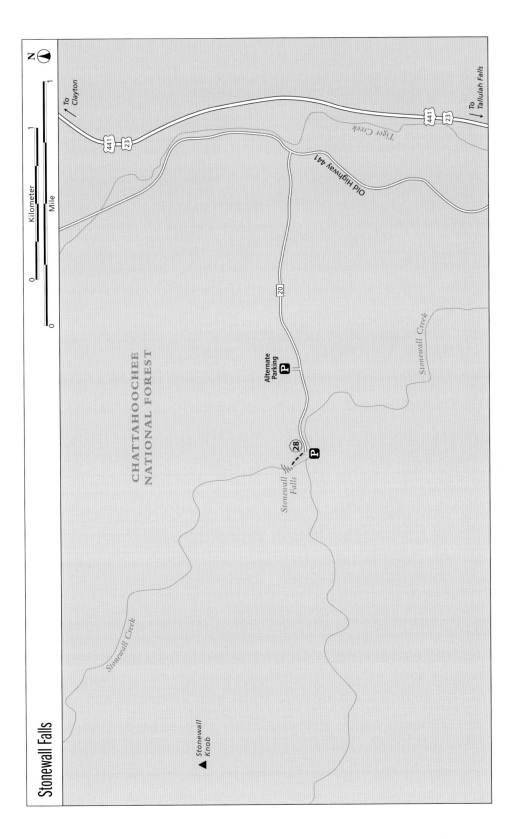

Ledge after ledge makes up Stonewall Falls. If your timing is right, you can camp right at the base of this beauty.

the Civil War who was arguably one of the best tactical commanders in U.S. history. Ironically, in 1863 he was accidentally shot by one of his own men. He survived the shooting with the amputation of one arm but then caught pneumonia, which led to his death eight days later.

29 Becky Branch Falls

Ticklish! The water of Becky Branch tap dances its way down the rocks, tickling the moss on its path to the base.

Height: 20 feet
Beauty rating: Very good
Distance: 0.4 mile out and back
Difficulty: Moderate
Trail surface: Hard-packed dirt
Approximate hiking time: 20 minutes
Blaze color: Yellow

County: Rabun
Land status: National forest
Trail contact: Chattahoochee National Forest, Chattooga Ranger District; (706) 754-6221; www.fs.fed.us
Maps: *DeLorme: Georgia Atlas & Gazetteer:* Page 16 C3

Finding the trailhead: From the junction of US 441 and US 76 east, drive north on US 441 for 0.25 mile. Turn right onto Warwoman Road (just north of the Day's Inn) and travel 2.8 miles to a right turn onto Warwoman Dell Lane at the sign for WARWOMAN DELL PICNIC AREA. Continue 0.1 mile down the hill; the parking area is on your left.

From the junction of US 441 and GA 246, drive south on US 441 for 7.4 miles. Turn left onto Warwoman Road (just north of the Day's Inn) and follow the directions above.

From the junction of Warwoman Road and GA 28, go west on Warwoman Road for 11.0 miles. Turn left onto Warwoman Dell Lane at the sign for WARWOMAN DELL PICNIC AREA and follow the directions above.

The trailhead is located to the west of the parking area, farther in on Warwoman Dell Lane. GPS: N34 52.950 / W83 21.053

The Hike

From the parking area, walk a few hundred feet farther in on the paved road; you will see the yellow-blazed Bartram Trail on your right, just past the tiny creek. This is the trailhead.

Head up the trail as it follows the creek upstream. The trail then makes a couple of quick switchbacks and leads to Warwoman Road. Cross the road and pick the trail up on the other side. From here, the trail rises steeply, following the creek upstream until you arrive at a wooden footbridge at the base of Becky Branch Falls.

Warwoman Dell, near which Becky Branch Falls lies, is named for the Cherokee woman Nancy Ward. According to the Cherokee, she was touted as the "last warwoman in the East." It is said that she fought side by side with her husband in the war against the Creek in 1755. When he was killed in battle, she took up his rifle and led the Cherokee to victory. Following the battle, she became known as *tsi-ge-yu,* Cherokee for "warwoman." Ward was so beloved and respected by her people that she was allowed to sit in on councils and to assist in making decisions for the tribe.

Becky Branch Falls and Martin Creek Falls

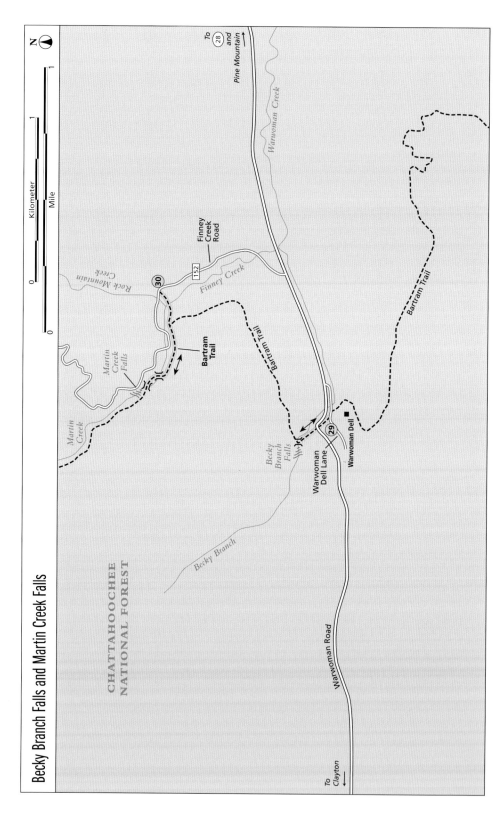

CHATTAHOOCHEE
NATIONAL FOREST

Martin Creek

Martin Creek Falls

Rock Mountain Creek

30

152

Finney Creek

Finney Creek Road

Bartram Trail

Bartram Trail

Becky Branch Falls

Becky Branch

Bartram Trail

Warwoman Dell Lane

29

Warwoman Dell

Warwoman Creek

Warwoman Road

To Clayton

To 28 and Pine Mountain

N

0   1   Kilometer
0   1   Mile

Daffodils return in greater numbers year after year.

Miles and Directions

0.0 From the trailhead, hike north, following the trail as it climbs and leads around a few switchbacks.

0.1 The trail reaches Warwoman Road. *Carefully* cross the road and continue hiking northwest as you begin to follow the creek upstream.

0.2 Arrive at the base of Becky Branch Falls (N34 53.046 / W83 21.146). Return the way you came.

0.4 Arrive back at the trailhead.

THE FIRST AMERICAN NATURALIST

William Bartram was perhaps the very first American-born naturalist and illustrator of nature. Bartram spent years traveling on foot, exploring the southeastern regions of the United States during the late 1700s. His travels began and ended in Philadelphia, Pennsylvania, where he was born, and he passed through eight states along the way.

As he made his way through the countryside, Bartram gathered and illustrated all the flora and fauna he could. He was one of the first people to draw and describe hundreds of plant, bird, and animal species. Bartram is not only famous for his collection of nature but is also credited for documenting the Native American tribes he encountered.

A trail named in his honor closely follows the paths taken by William Bartram himself more than 200 years ago. A well-marked, 37-mile portion of the Bartram Trail runs throughout the mountains of north Georgia. For a wealth of information regarding the man, his travels, and the trail that bears his name, visit www.bartramtrail.org.

30 Martin Creek Falls

Playful! On the Author's Favorites List, Martin Creek Falls is a perfect place to frolic in the water as it spills over the stones in the creek.

See map on page 104.
Height: 40 feet
Beauty rating: Excellent
Distance: 1.0 mile out and back
Difficulty: Easy to moderate
Trail surface: Hard-packed dirt
Approximate hiking time: 40 minutes
Blaze color: Yellow

County: Rabun
Land status: National forest
Trail contact: Chattahoochee National Forest, Chattooga Ranger District; (706) 754-6221; www.fs.fed.us
Maps: *DeLorme: Georgia Atlas & Gazetteer:* Page 16 B3

Finding the trailhead: From the junction of US 441 and US 76 east, drive north on US 441 for 0.25 mile. Turn right onto Warwoman Road (just north of the Day's Inn) and travel 3.4 miles to a left turn onto Finney Creek Road (FS 152). Continue for 0.4 mile just past the small creek to where the road makes a sharp left turn and heads uphill. Just before this left turn, look to your left and see a small pull-in to what used to be a camping area.

From the junction of US 441 and GA 246, drive south on US 441 for 7.4 miles. Turn left onto Warwoman Road (just north of the Day's Inn) and follow the directions above.

From the junction of Warwoman Road and GA 28, go west on Warwoman Road for 10.4 miles. Turn right onto Finney Creek Road (FS 152) and follow the directions above.

The trailhead is located at the southwest corner of the parking area. GPS: N34 53.513 / W83 20.562

The Hike

Follow the very overgrown, narrow dirt path into the woods and soon come to an obscure trail forking off to the right. Take this side trail to the right, which quickly leads to the creek. Cross the creek and follow the nearly nonexistent trail diagonally and up to the right (west) for approximately 0.1 mile. Once at the top of the hill, the trail unites with the larger and more defined yellow-blazed Bartram Trail.

Go right onto the Bartram Trail and follow it upstream along the creekside. After passing some primitive campsites, you soon see a small wooden footbridge on your right that goes across Martin Creek. Cross the footbridge and continue upstream and uphill, still following the narrow yellow-blazed footpath. A short distance farther, cross another wooden footbridge, which leads to an observation deck at the base of the very playful Martin Creek Falls.

Located along the Bartram Trail, Martin Creek won't disappoint.

In William Bartram's day, this was known as Falling Branch Falls. It later came to be known as Martin Creek Falls for Gen. Joseph Martin, who served in the legislatures of Georgia, North Carolina, and Virginia. Due to his close ties with the Cherokee, he is said to have played an integral part in our success in the Revolutionary War.

Close ties indeed. One of his five wives was the Cherokee Princess Elizabeth "Betsy" Ward, daughter of the famous "warwoman" Nancy Ward.

Miles and Directions

0.0 From the trailhead, a very overgrown, narrow dirt path heads southwest into the woods. Take this path and quickly come to an obscure fork. Go right at this fork, continuing west on the overgrown path until you come to a small creek. Cross the creek and head right as you make your way farther west.

0.1 The trail begins to climb and joins the yellow-blazed Bartram Trail. Go right onto the Bartram Trail, following the creek upstream and generally west.

0.3 After passing some primitive campsites, rock-hop a small tributary and continue northwest until you come to a wooden footbridge. Cross the footbridge and continue hiking north, upstream and uphill.

0.5 Cross another footbridge, which leads south to an observation deck at the base of Martin Creek Falls (N34 53.568 / W83 20.960). Return the way you came.

1.0 Arrive back at the trailhead.

31 Dick's Creek Falls

Amazing! Dick's Creek is unique in that it flows directly into the Wild and Scenic Chattooga River. From the base of the falls, the creek pushes out into Section III of the Chattooga to Dick's Creek Ledge, a Class III+ rapid. You'll be entranced by the beauty and strength of both the waterfall and the river here.

Height: 60 feet
Beauty rating: Excellent
Distance: 1.2 miles out and back
Difficulty: Easy
Trail surface: Hard-packed dirt
Approximate hiking time: 30 minutes
Blaze color: No blazes

County: Rabun
Land status: National forest
Trail contact: Chattahoochee National Forest, Chattooga Ranger District; (706) 754-6221; www.fs.fed.us
Maps: *DeLorme: Georgia Atlas & Gazetteer:* Page 16 C4

Finding the trailhead: From the junction of US 441 and US 76 east, drive north on US 441 for 0.25 mile. Turn right onto Warwoman Road (just north of the Day's Inn) and travel 5.7 miles to a right turn onto Sandy Ford Road. Follow Sandy Ford Road for 0.65 mile to an intersection with John Houck Road. Stay left here, crossing the bridge and continuing on Sandy Ford Road until you have gone a total of 3.9 miles from Warwoman Road. At 3.9 miles you will see a creek ford in front of you and a small pull-off on the left (east) side of the road before the ford.

From the junction of US 441 and GA 246, drive south on US 441 for 7.4 miles. Turn left onto Warwoman Road (just north of the Day's Inn) and follow the directions above.

From the junction of Warwoman Road and GA 28, drive west on Warwoman Road for 3.9 miles. Turn left onto Sandy Ford Road and follow the directions above.

The trailhead for the Dick's Creek Falls Trail (#60) heads east from the pull-off and into the woods. GPS: N34 52.240/W83 15.196

The Hike

Begin hiking on the old roadbed as it follows the small creek downstream for a short distance. The roadlike path soon narrows and becomes a dirt path. Continue on the easily followed path as it bends left and then brings you to a small tributary crossing. After crossing the tributary, head right, continuing deeper into the forest to an intersection with the yellow-blazed Bartram Trail.

Go straight across this trail and cross a small wooden footbridge. A short distance downstream from the footbridge, you arrive at the brink of Dick's Creek Falls. Continue a bit farther downstream and soon find yourself in awe as the scenery before you unfolds. Breathtaking views of the river fill you with inspiration.

Dick's Creek Falls flows directly into Section III of the Chattooga River.

As you make your way downhill from the brink, you will see a trail forking off to the right (southwest) toward the river. Take this trail and soon arrive at the base of Dick's Creek Falls, where the creek quickly rushes out to meet the river.

The famed Chattooga River forms the state line between Georgia and South Carolina, although prior to 1816, the state line sat farther east in South Carolina. The boundary was extended through a treaty with the Cherokee, moving the state line to its current location along the river's edge.

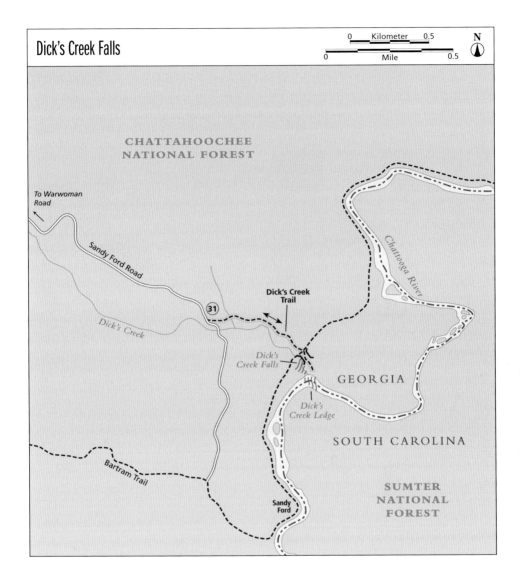

0   Kilometer   0.5   N

0   Mile   0.5

CHATTAHOOCHEE
NATIONAL FOREST

To Warwoman
Road

Sandy Ford Road

Dick's Creek
Trail

31

Dick's Creek

Dick's
Creek Falls

Chattooga River

GEORGIA

Dick's
Creek Ledge

SOUTH CAROLINA

Bartram Trail

Sandy
Ford

SUMTER
NATIONAL
FOREST

Miles and Directions

0.0 From the trailhead, head east into the woods on the old roadbed as it follows the small creek downstream. The wide roadlike path soon becomes a narrow dirt path.

0.1 The trail leads to a small tributary. Cross the tributary and head right (east) as you make your way deeper into the forest.

0.3 Come to a fork with a small trail shooting off to the right. This is just a spur trail around some downed trees. Bypass it, continuing to follow the main trail. Make your way over the logs and continue heading east on the Dick's Creek Falls Trail.

Dick's Creek Ledge, a Class III+ rapid on the Wild and Scenic Chattooga River, sits near the base of Dick's Creek Falls.

0.4 Come to an intersection with the yellow-blazed Bartram Trail. Go straight (southeast) across the Bartram Trail and immediately cross a small footbridge. Continue hiking southeast.

0.5 Reach the brink of the falls. As you head downstream and downhill (southeast) from the brink, you will see a trail that forks off to the right (southwest) toward the river. Take this trail down toward the river.

0.6 Arrive at the Chattooga River at the base of Dick's Creek Falls (N34 52.059 / W83 14.760). Return the way you came.

1.2 Arrive back at the trailhead.

32 Holcomb and Ammons Falls

Twice the pleasure! First you are greeted with massive and mighty Holcomb Falls, towering overhead and flowing with great strength and force. This power is soon followed by the extremely calming waters of Ammons Falls.

Height: Holcomb Falls, 120 feet; Ammons Falls, 40 feet
Beauty rating: Very good
Distance: 1.0 mile out and back (Holcomb Falls, 0.6 mile)
Difficulty: Moderate to strenuous
Trail surface: Hard-packed dirt
Approximate hiking time: 40 minutes

Blaze color: No blazes
County: Rabun
Land status: National forest
Trail contact: Chattahoochee National Forest, Chattooga Ranger District; (706) 754-6221; www.fs.fed.us
Maps: *DeLorme: Georgia Atlas & Gazetteer:* Page 16 A4

Finding the trailhead: From the junction of US 441 and US 76 east, drive north on US 441 for 0.25 mile. Turn right turn onto Warwoman Road (just north of the Day's Inn) and travel 9.8 miles to a left turn onto Hale Ridge Road. Follow Hale Ridge Road for 6.5 miles to where it intersects Overflow Creek Road. There is a pull-off on the right, just before this intersection.

From the junction of US 441 and GA 246, drive south on US 441 for 7.4 miles. Turn left onto Warwoman Road (just north of the Day's Inn) and follow the directions above.

From the junction of Warwoman Road and GA 28, drive west on Warwoman Road for 4.7 miles. Turn right onto Hale Ridge Road and follow the directions above.

The trailhead is northwest of the parking area on the north side of Overflow Creek Road, marked by a blue ring around a tree and a large stone with Holcomb Creek Trail etched into it. GPS: N34 58.720 / W83 15.980

The Hike

From the trailhead, Holcomb Creek Trail (#52) descends rapidly into the stillness of the woods. Follow it around a few switchbacks and come to a wooden footbridge. Cross the bridge and continue on the evident path as it takes you on a downhill journey to a bridge at the base of Holcomb Falls.

From Holcomb Falls, cross the bridge and see a sign for Ammons Falls. Head right at the sign and downstream. The trail leads back into the woods and then heads up and to the left on the now clearer path. As you make the steep climb, be sure to bypass the side trail on your left (it leads to Hale Ridge Road about 0.6 mile from where you parked). Instead stay on the main trail, continuing your ascent until you reach the observation deck at the base of the calming waters of Ammons Falls.

Holcomb Falls is a pleasant surprise every time.

Although they are located along the same trail, these two waterfalls are actually on separate creeks: Holcomb and Ammons. I was able to find evidence of a Holcomb family in Rabun County during the Civil War and as far back as 1805 in nearby Habersham County. But I could find no significant data as to why they would have a creek named for them. The same goes for Ammons, although there is a headstone at the Hale Ridge Cemetery reading YOUNG AMMONS, with no dates provided.

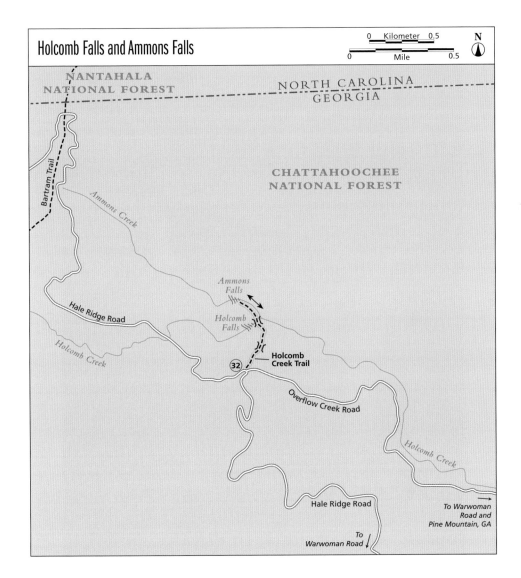

Holcomb Falls and Ammons Falls

0   Kilometer   0.5

0   Mile   0.5

N

NANTAHALA
NATIONAL FOREST

NORTH CAROLINA
GEORGIA

CHATTAHOOCHEE
NATIONAL FOREST

Bartram Trail

Ammons Creek

Ammons
Falls

Hale Ridge Road

Holcomb
Falls

Holcomb Creek

32

Holcomb
Creek Trail

Overflow Creek Road

Holcomb Creek

Hale Ridge Road

To Warwoman
Road and
Pine Mountain, GA

To
Warwoman Road

Miles and Directions

0.0 From the trailhead, hike north into the forest. The trail makes a rapid descent around a few switchbacks.

0.1 Cross a wooden footbridge and continue hiking northeast on the evident footpath as you continue downhill.

0.3 Arrive at a bridge at the base of Holcomb Falls (N34 58.906/W83 15.933). (*Option:* Turn around here for a 0.6 mile hike.)To continue to Ammons Falls, cross the bridge and head right (north-northeast). Continue back into the woods, where the trail bends left (north-west) and begins to climb.

Following a strenuous climb, the cool, damp air from Ammons Falls is quite a refreshing treat.

0.5 As you make the steep climb, bypass the trail on the left (south). (This trail leads back to Hale Ridge Road about 0.6 mile from where you parked.) Continue straight ahead (northwest) on the Holcomb Creek Trail and soon arrive at an observation deck at the base of Ammons Falls (N34 59.005/W83 16.009). Return the way you came.

1.0 Arrive back at the trailhead.

33 Ada-Hi Falls

Aspiring! Like a weeping wall, Ada-Hi Falls is more of a trickle than a waterfall. The water almost appears to seep from the rock face. The spring that feeds this simple fall is a mere 300 feet above the waterfall, so it doesn't have time to collect the momentum and volume that most other falls have. Although the waterfall itself is not much to see, the trail and road to the trailhead are excellent for viewing a variety of wildflowers.

Height: 35 feet
Beauty rating: Fair
Distance: 0.6 mile out and back
Difficulty: Moderate
Trail surface: Mulch path
Approximate hiking time: 20 minutes
Blaze color: No blazes

County: Rabun
Land status: State park
Trail contact: Black Rock Mountain State Park; (706) 746-2141; www.gastateparks.org
FYI: Open 7 a.m. to 10 p.m.
Maps: *DeLorme: Georgia Atlas & Gazetteer:* Page 16 B3

Finding the trailhead: From the junction of US 441 and US 76 east, drive north on US 441 for 3.0 miles. Turn left onto Black Rock Mountain Parkway at the First Christian Church and head up the mountain. At approximately 1.0 mile you will see a large sign for Black Rock Mountain State Park on the left. Do not turn left here. Instead continue straight ahead, still heading up the mountain until you reach the gate at the entrance to the park. Enter the park and continue up the mountain until you come to a fork. Go left at the fork, following the signs a short distance to the campground entrance. There's a small parking area on the right just before the campground office.

From the junction of US 441 and GA 246, drive south on US 441 for 4.6 miles. Turn right onto Black Rock Mountain Parkway at the First Christian Church and follow the directions above.

The trailhead is located just before the campground office, on the east side of the road. GPS: N34 54.381 / W83 24.462

The Hike

The obvious mulch path rapidly descends a fairly steep grade into the forest. Not to worry though; there are benches along the path where you can rest on your way out, and the abundance of wildflowers along the path makes it worth every step. The trail leads across a small footbridge and then down multiple levels of steps to an observation deck at Ada-Hi Falls.

Named for the Cherokee word for "forest," Ada-Hi sits at the highest elevation of any waterfall in Georgia. This makes sense being that it is located within Black Rock Mountain State Park, at 3,640 feet Georgia's highest-elevation state park. The park is named for the sheer cliffs of dark-colored biotite gneiss, which seem far more impressive than Ada-Hi Falls. On a clear day you can see four states (Georgia, North Carolina, South Carolina, and Tennessee) from atop Black Rock Mountain.

Ada-Hi Falls and Sylvan Mill Falls

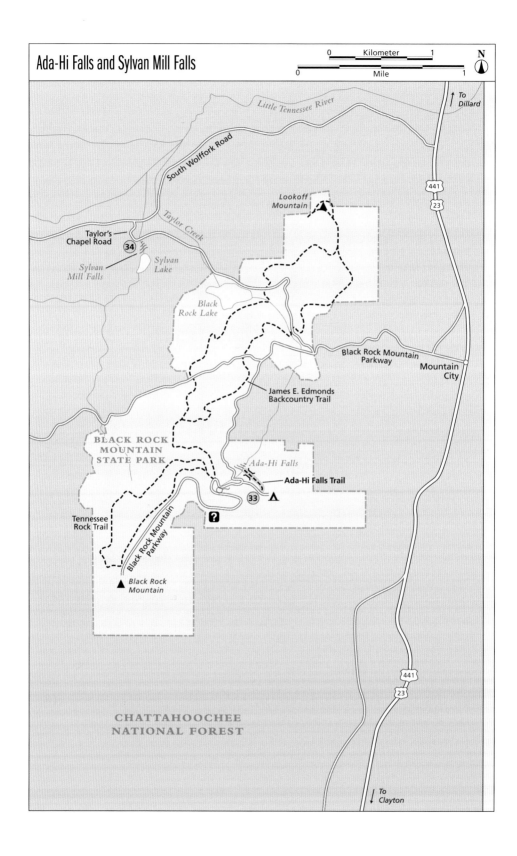

Kilometer

Mile

N

To Dillard

Little Tennessee River

South Wolffork Road

441

23

Taylor Creek

Lookoff Mountain

Taylor's Chapel Road

34

Sylvan Mill Falls

Sylvan Lake

Black Rock Lake

Black Rock Mountain Parkway

Mountain City

James E. Edmonds Backcountry Trail

23

BLACK ROCK MOUNTAIN STATE PARK

Ada-Hi Falls

Ada-Hi Falls Trail

33

?

Tennessee Rock Trail

Black Rock Mountain Parkway

Black Rock Mountain

CHATTAHOOCHEE NATIONAL FOREST

441

23

To Clayton

Miles and Directions

0.0 From the trailhead, the obvious mulch path descends southeast on a fairly steep grade.

0.2 The trail takes you across a small footbridge and then down many levels of steps.

0.3 Arrive at the base of Ada-Hi Falls (N34 54.482 / W83 24.568). Return the way you came.

0.6 Arrive back at the trailhead.

WHERE THE WATER SPLITS

The Eastern Continental Divide (ECD) is an imaginary line where the water "splits" and flows in either one direction or the other. The ECD primarily follows the ridgeline and high peaks of the Appalachian Mountain Range.

Simply put, all the streams, creeks, and rivers east of the divide eventually flow from one to the next until they make their way out to the Atlantic Ocean. All the water flowing on the west side of the ECD either flows directly into the Gulf of Mexico or to the Mississippi River, which then carries it out to the Gulf of Mexico.

Much like the mountain laurel, the native touch-me-not blossoms spring open and toss out their pollen when touched.

34 Sylvan Mill Falls

Pristine! Sylvan Mill Falls is a wonderful treat for a roadside waterfall. A picturesque scene, straight out of a fairy tale, is perfectly painted here.

See map on page 118.
Height: 50 feet
Beauty rating: Excellent
Distance: Roadside
Difficulty: Easy
Blaze color: No blazes

County: Rabun
Land status: Private property
Trail contact: Sylvan Falls Mill Bed and Breakfast; (706) 746-7138; www.sylvanfallsmill.com
Maps: *DeLorme: Georgia Atlas & Gazetteer:* Page 16 B2

Finding the trailhead: From the junction of US 441 and US 76 east, drive north on US 441 for 4.25 miles. Turn left onto South Wolffork Road across from the gas station and travel 2.2 miles to a left turn onto Taylor's Chapel Road. Continue for 0.2 mile to view the falls on the right.

From the junction of US 441 and GA 246, drive south on US 441 for 3.3 miles. Turn right onto South Wolffork Road across from the gas station. (Be sure to travel the full 3.3 miles so that you don't mistakenly turn onto North Wolffork Road.) After turning onto South Wolffork Road, follow the directions above.

GPS: N34 55.651 / W83 25.239

The Hike

Sylvan Mill Falls can be viewed from the roadside.

The bed-and-breakfast that gives this waterfall a home has lovely gardens that sit at the base of the falls and a wonderful water wheel to the right. At 27 feet, it is one of the largest waterwheels in the United States and has been in operation for 168 years. Once a thriving gristmill, the mill still grinds flour today for use in the B&B.

If you're in the area, a quick visit to this neighborhood waterfall is worth the trip. Or perhaps you'll opt to stay at the eco-friendly Sylvan Falls Mill Bed and Breakfast, which proudly uses "local, regional, organic and sustainable" products.

Sylvan Mill Falls has a working waterwheel and is graced with gardens galore.

THE 100-MILE RULE

More and more people in today's eco-friendly society are becoming aware of their "carbon footprint." One way to reduce your footprint is to try to live by the "100-Mile Rule," which encourages people to try to "eat local." The idea is to purchase only products that are grown, raised, or made within 100 miles of your home.

Local produce is fresher, animals are range fed, and it supports the local economy. You are not only helping the environment but are making an investment in your health as well. While it can be difficult to eat 100 percent local, every little bit helps. Keep this in mind the next time you step into the grocery store.

35 Eastatoah Falls

Panache! This roadside beauty stands tall on the mountainside but oft times goes unnoticed. The stretch of highway that Eastatoah Falls keeps watch over is not very "parking friendly," so use caution, and keep your roadside visit brief.

See overview map on page iv.
Height: 200 feet
Beauty rating: Good
Distance: Roadside
Difficulty: Easy
Blaze color: No blazes

County: Rabun
Land status: Private property
Trail contact: None
Maps: *DeLorme: Georgia Atlas & Gazetteer:* Page 16 A3; *DeLorme: North Carolina Atlas & Gazetteer:* Page 51 F7

Finding the trailhead: From the junction of US 441 and US 76 east, drive north on US 441 for 7.7 miles. Turn right onto GA 246 and drive approximately 1.5 miles to a small pull-off on the left.

From the Georgia–North Carolina state line, drive south on US 441 for 0.7 mile. Turn left onto GA 246 and follow the directions above.

GPS: N34 59.459 / W83 21.543

The Hike

Eastatoah Falls can be viewed from the roadside. From the pull-off, look east to get a glimpse of the falls flowing down the mountainside in the distance. I recommend bringing binoculars or a good zoom lens if you really want to appreciate this one. Also known as Falls on Ford Mountain and Falls on Mud Creek, this one is located on private property, so the best you can do is view it from afar.

Some waterfalls are viewed from afar—others you can reach out and touch.

One reasonable theory for the name is that it comes from the Cherokee village of Eastertoy, which was located in the town of Sky Valley, near present-day Dillard, Georgia. Over the years, *Eastertoy* became *Eastatoah*.

South Carolina
Waterfalls

Wildlife abounds on the trail to Opossum Creek Falls (hike 39).

36 Bull Sluice

Serene! This Class V rapid along Section III of the Wild and Scenic Chattooga River falls and flows perfectly over the rocky-bottomed river floor. With strength and serenity, it holds your gaze.

Height: 10 feet
Beauty rating: Very good
Distance: 0.4 mile out and back
Difficulty: Easy
Trail surface: Paved path and gravel trail
Approximate hiking time: 20 minutes
Blaze color: No blazes
County: Rabun, Georgia; Oconee, South Carolina

Land status: National forest
Trail contacts: Chattahoochee National Forest, Chattooga Ranger District; (706) 754-6221; www.fs.fed.us
  Sumter National Forest, Andrew Pickens Ranger District; (864) 638-9568; www.fs.fed.us
Maps: *DeLorme: South Carolina Atlas & Gazetteer:* Page 16 B1; *DeLorme: Georgia Atlas & Gazetteer:* Page 16 D4

Finding the trailhead: From the junction of US 76 east and US 441, drive east on US 76 for 8.2 miles. Just after crossing the Chattooga River Bridge, pull into a parking area on the left signed for the HIGHWAY 76 CHATTOOGA RIVER ACCESS AREA.

From the junction of US 76 and US 123, drive west on US 76 for 17.7 miles. Just before crossing the Chattooga River Bridge, pull into a parking area on the right signed for the HIGHWAY 76 CHATTOOGA RIVER ACCESS AREA.

The trailhead is located next to the large pavilion at the north end of the parking lot. GPS: N34 48.905 / W83 18.306

The Hike

From the trailhead, follow the wide, paved path as it leads downhill and toward the river. Approximately 0.1 mile down the hill, a gravel trail shoots off to the right. Take this trail and follow it for another 0.1 mile as it leads to the Chattooga River at the base of the powerful rapid known as Bull Sluice.

For a quick side trip, backtrack to the paved path and continue to follow it downhill to where it comes out at a lovely sandy beach alongside the river. This beach is the launch site for river rafters as they head out to paddle Section IV of the Chattooga River.

Bull Sluice is located within a 15.7-mile stretch of the Chattooga that has been protected since the spring of 1974. The river proudly has national forest on both sides, giving it a wonderful buffer zone on which no commercial roads or development is allowed.

▶ Each rapid in a river is classified on a standardized scale according to difficulty. The International Scale of River Difficulty ranges from the tamest Class I rapid to the most difficult, often "unrunnable," Class VI.

Bull Sluice

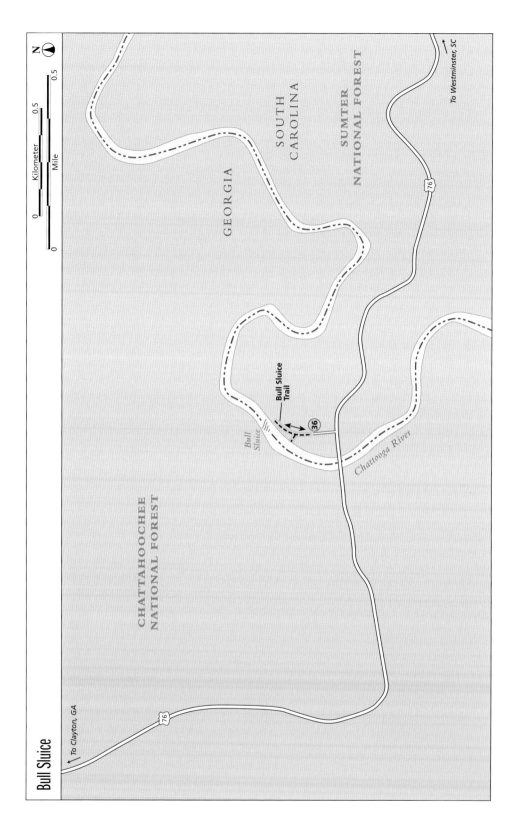

You might be lucky enough to see river rafters and kayakers run the Class V rapid known as Bull Sluice.

It is said that the rocks that make up the riverbed were carved out over a span of 600 to 750 million years.

Miles and Directions

0.0 From the trailhead, hike north down the paved path as it heads downhill and toward the river.

0.1 Reach a junction with a gravel trail off to the right (northeast). Follow this trail as it leads back into the woods from above the river.

0.2 Arrive at the river's edge at the base of Bull Sluice (N34 49.027 / W83 18.276). Return the way you came.

0.4 Arrive back at the trailhead.

37 Fall Creek Falls

Inspiring! Like the wings of a dove flapping in the wind, Fall Creek Falls brings a similar offering of peace.

Height: 60 feet
Beauty rating: Very good
Distance: 0.2 mile out and back
Difficulty: Moderate
Trail surface: Hard-packed dirt
Approximate hiking time: 20 minutes
Blaze color: No blazes
County: Oconee

Land status: National forest
Trail contact: Sumter National Forest, Andrew Pickens Ranger District; (864) 638-9568; www.fs.fed.us
Maps: *DeLorme: South Carolina Atlas & Gazetteer:* Page 16 H1; *DeLorme: Georgia Atlas & Gazetteer:* Page 16 C4

Finding the trailhead: From the junction of US 76 and US 441 in Clayton, Georgia, drive east on US 76 for 10.0 miles. Turn left onto Chattooga Ridge Road and travel 2.0 miles to a left turn onto Fall Creek Road. Continue for 0.3 mile and turn left onto Fall Creek Road Extension (FS 722). Travel 0.5 mile to a small pull-off on the left, just after crossing a tiny stream that you can hear but not see.

From the junction of US 76 and the Chattooga River Bridge (Georgia–South Carolina state line), drive east on US 76 for 2.0 miles. Turn left onto Chattooga Ridge Road and follow the directions above.

From the junction of US 76 and US 123, drive west on US 76 for 15.2 miles. Turn right onto Chattooga Ridge Road and follow the directions above.

GPS: N34 49.363 / W83 15.049

The Hike

From the pull off you will see a narrow path that leads steeply downhill to the creek. Follow the path downstream for a very short distance to reach the brink of the falls. Continue steeply down into the woods just a little bit farther until you reach the creek at the base of Fall Creek Falls. For the best view, rock-hop out into the creek.

Aptly named, Fall Creek is home to not just one, but three cascades over a 1.0-mile stretch of creek. Each, however, is more difficult and challenging to reach than the one before. For this reason, I have only showcased the first.

Fall Creek Falls and Falls on Reedy Branch

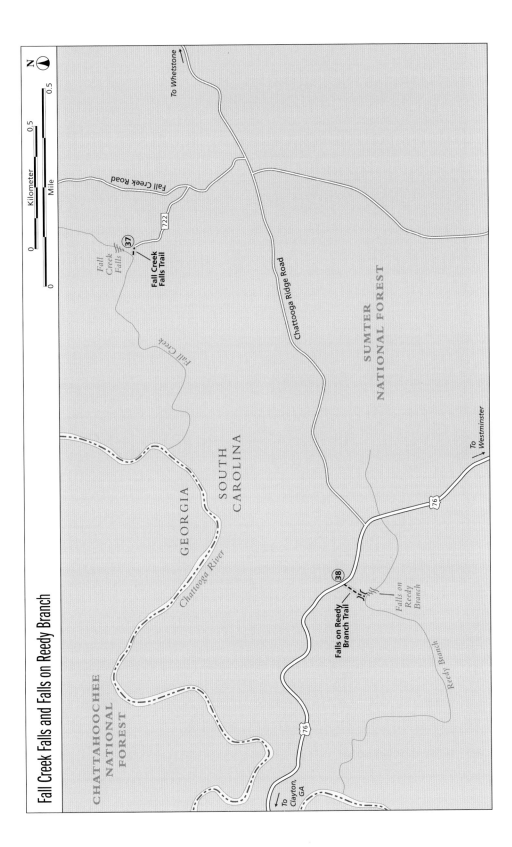

To Whetstone

Fall Creek Road

722

37
Fall Creek Falls
Fall Creek Falls Trail

Fall Creek

Chattooga Ridge Road

SUMTER NATIONAL FOREST

CHATTAHOOCHEE NATIONAL FOREST

Chattooga River

GEORGIA
SOUTH CAROLINA

To Westminster

76

38
Falls on Reedy Branch Trail

Falls on Reedy Branch

Reedy Branch

76

To Clayton, GA

N

Kilometer
0   0.5
0   0.5
Mile

Standing up straight and tall, Fall Creek Falls outshines them all.

Miles and Directions

0.0 From the trailhead, hike south-southwest on the narrow path as it leads steeply downhill to the creek. Follow the creek downstream for a very short distance to reach the brink of the falls.

0.1 Continue more steeply down into the woods until you reach the creek at the base of Fall Creek Falls (N34 49.368 / W83 15.084). Return the way you came.

0.2 Arrive back at the trailhead.

38 Falls on Reedy Branch

Mysterious! A gorgeous gazebo alongside the base of the falls makes you wonder who once lived here. It feels as though you are trespassing as you pass through the stone pillars at the trailhead, heading down the driveway to what may have been someone's dream home.

See map on page 129.
Height: 60 feet
Beauty rating: Very good
Distance: 0.4 mile out and back
Difficulty: Easy to moderate
Trail surface: Wide old roadbed and narrow footpath
Approximate hiking time: 20 minutes
Blaze color: No blazes

County: Oconee
Land status: National forest
Trail contact: Sumter National Forest, Andrew Pickens Ranger District; (864) 638-9568; www.fs.fed.us
Maps: *DeLorme: South Carolina Atlas & Gazetteer:* Page 22 A1; *DeLorme: Georgia Atlas & Gazetteer:* Page 16 D4

Finding the trailhead: From the junction of US 76 and US 441 in Clayton, Georgia, drive east on US 76 for 9.8 miles to a pull-off on the right next to a low stone wall. This is the beginning of FS 2751.

From the junction of US 76 and the Chattooga River Bridge (Georgia–South Carolina state line), drive east on US 76 for 1.7 miles to a pull-off on the right next to a low stone wall.

From the junction of US 76 and US 123, drive west on US 76 for 15.5 miles to a pull-off on the left next to a low stone wall.

The trailhead is located at the stone pillars at the south end of the parking area. GPS: N34 48.444 / W83 16.858

The Hike

Begin the hike by going around the stone pillars and following FS 2751 downhill. As you reach the bottom of the hill, you will see a small side trail on the left just before the road crosses a small stone bridge. Take this side trail, following it over a small wooden footbridge. Continue a short distance farther to arrive at the base of the Falls on Reedy Branch.

I was enjoying a cold beverage at the nearby Bonnie Blue Saloon, just east of the trailhead, when a patron shared this one with me. *Thanks!*

The area surrounding the falls was in the midst of a development project when it was acquired by the Sumter National Forest, leaving that dream home, at least for some, just a dream.

Falls on Reedy Branch are flawless as they flow into their own hidden cove.

Miles and Directions

0.0 From the trailhead, go around the stone pillars and hike south on the old roadbed, making your way downhill.

0.2 At the bottom of the hill, come to a side trail on the left before FS 2751 heads over a stone bridge. Go left (south) on this side trail, which crosses a footbridge before quickly leading to the base of Falls on Reedy Branch (N34 48.323 / W83 16.896). Return the way you came.

0.4 Arrive back at the trailhead

39 Opossum Creek Falls

Stupendous! With its brilliant, milky-white water, Opossum Creek Falls warms the heart and soul. Its mossy face and spongy touch make this waterfall truly an amazing thing to see and feel. Easily on the Author's Favorites List, this is one of my choice spots to spend a day.

Height: 120 feet
Beauty rating: Excellent
Distance: 5.0 miles out and back
Difficulty: Moderate to strenuous
Trail surface: Hard-packed dirt
Approximate hiking time: 2 hours, 30 minutes
Blaze color: No blazes
County: Oconee

Land status: National forest
Trail contact: Sumter National Forest, Andrew Pickens Ranger District; (864) 638-9568; www.fs.fed.us
Maps: *DeLorme: South Carolina Atlas & Gazetteer:* Page 16 B1; *DeLorme: Georgia Atlas & Gazetteer:* Page 16 D4

Finding the trailhead: From the junction of US 76 and US 441 in Clayton, Georgia, drive east on US 76 for 12.4 miles. Turn right at the fire station onto Damascus Church Road and travel 0.8 mile to a fork in the road. Go right at the fork onto Battle Creek Road and continue for 1.8 miles. Turn right onto Turkey Ridge Road (FS 755) and travel 2.1 miles to a pull-off on the left next to FS 755F.

From the junction of US 76 and the Chattooga River Bridge (Georgia–South Carolina state line), drive east on US 76 for 4.4 miles. Turn right at the fire station onto Damascus Church Road and follow the directions above.

From the junction of US 76 and US 123, drive west on US 76 for 12.8 miles. Turn left at the fire station onto Damascus Church Road and follow the directions above.

The trailhead is located on the west side of the road, approximately 200 feet south of the pull-off. GPS: N34 46.404 / W83 18.255

The Hike

From where you parked, walk back south on FS 755 for approximately 200 feet to reach the trailhead on the west side of the road. The obvious trail heads south, down into the woods. The easily followed trail makes its way around some switchbacks and reaches the forest floor after about 0.3 mile. Once on the forest floor, the trail narrows and meanders generally southwest and west through the forest for approximately 0.75 mile.

The trail begins to climb slightly before heading primarily downhill for the next 1.1 miles. After the descent you arrive at Opossum Creek as it flows out into the Chattooga River directly in front of you. Crossing this creek will not take you to the waterfall, but it will take you to a wonderful sandy beach along the Chattooga River—a nice little side trip while you're out here.

White-tailed deer are commonly seen at dawn or dusk.

To get to Opossum Creek Falls, do not cross the creek. Instead head left (southeast) and follow the creek upstream for another 0.3 mile. The narrow overgrown path requires rock-hopping a couple of small tributaries before you arrive at the base of Opossum Creek Falls.

The forest surrounding the trail to Opossum Creek Falls provides an excellent habitat for wild turkey, bobcat, and black bear. While I've yet to see the latter two, I have had the pleasure of seeing wild turkey here on many occasions.

OPPORTUNISTIC OPOSSUMS

Opossums are nocturnal creatures that are often misunderstood due to their scary looks and mouth full of teeth. Typically slow-moving and passive animals, when cornered they'll usually just play dead, or "possum," as a defense mechanism.

People often fear them as carriers of rabies, but actually it is very rare for an opossum to be infected with the virus. You are far more likely to become infected by a cute and cuddly raccoon than by an ominous-looking opossum.

These marsupials are well adapted to a wide variety of habitats and are opportunistic omnivores, eating just about anything they can get their paws on.

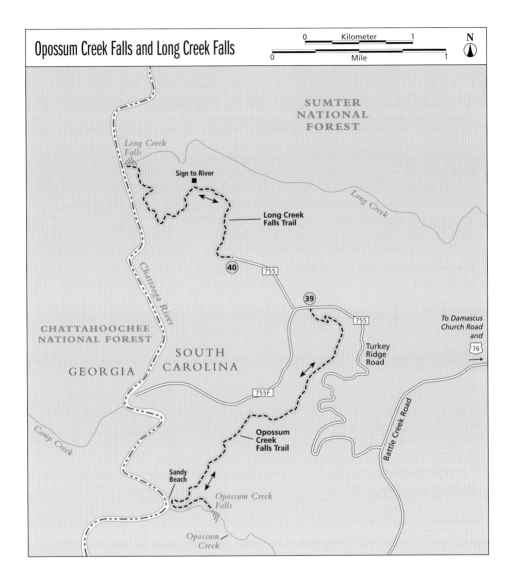

Opossum Creek Falls and Long Creek Falls

SUMTER NATIONAL FOREST

Long Creek Falls

Sign to River

Long Creek Falls Trail

Long Creek

Chattooga River

40 755

39 755

To Damascus Church Road and 76

CHATTAHOOCHEE NATIONAL FOREST

GEORGIA

SOUTH CAROLINA

Turkey Ridge Road

755F

Battle Creek Road

Camp Creek

Opossum Creek Falls Trail

Sandy Beach

Opossum Creek Falls

Opossum Creek

Miles and Directions

0.0 From the trailhead, hike south on the obvious trail as you make your way downhill and into the forest.

2.2 Come to a creek crossing next to the river. Do not cross the creek; instead go left (southeast) and follow Opossum Creek upstream on the narrow overgrown path.

2.5 Arrive at the base of Opossum Creek Falls (N34 45.434 / W83 18.859). Return the way you came.

5.0 Arrive back at the trailhead.

40 Long Creek Falls

Perfection! Long Creek Falls is like two ladies dancing under the moonlight, enticing you to cast your gaze upon them and then not allowing you to look away. On the Author's Favorites list, this one will not disappoint.

See map on page 135.
Height: 40 feet
Beauty rating: Excellent
Distance: 3.8 miles out and back
Difficulty: Moderate to strenuous
Trail surface: Wide old roadbed; narrow hard-packed dirt
Approximate hiking time: 2 hours
Blaze color: No blazes

County: Oconee
Land status: National forest
Trail contact: Sumter National Forest, Andrew Pickens Ranger District; (864) 638-9568; www.fs.fed.us
Maps: *DeLorme: South Carolina Atlas & Gazetteer:* Page 16 B1; *DeLorme: Georgia Atlas & Gazetteer:* Page 16 D4

Finding the trailhead: From the junction of US 76 and US 441 in Clayton, Georgia, drive east on US 76 for 12.4 miles. Turn right at the fire station onto Damascus Church Road and travel 0.8 mile to a fork in the road. Go right at the fork onto Battle Creek Road and continue for 1.8 miles to Turkey Ridge Road (FS 755). Turn right onto Turkey Ridge Road and travel 2.8 miles to where the road dead-ends. (**Note:** As you follow Turkey Ridge Road, be sure to bypass FS 755F on your left.)

From the junction of US 76 and the Chattooga River Bridge (Georgia–South Carolina state line), drive east on US 76 for 4.4 miles. Turn right at the fire station onto Damascus Church Road and follow the directions above.

From the junction of US 76 and US 123, drive west on US 76 for 12.8 miles. Turn left at the fire station onto Damascus Church Road and follow the directions above.

The trailhead is located where FS 755, now a wide dirt path, continues into the woods on the right. GPS: N34 46.663 / W83 18.734

The Hike

From the parking area you will see where the old FS 755 roadbed continues down and into the woods on your right. This is the trailhead. Follow the wide and bumpy roadbed down into the forest until you come to a fork in the road. Stay right, following the trail until it dead-ends at a second fork with two old roadbeds. Bear right here as well, following the less-overgrown roadbed downhill.

Shortly after entering the woods, the roadbed narrows into a footpath. Continue straight ahead, following the trail as it winds through the forest. Bypass the obscure side trails off to the left as you hear the river down below. Continue hiking until you've gone a total of 1.5 miles and see a more obvious side trail heading down and to the left (northwest). Follow this side trail as it makes a steep descent toward the Chattooga River.

The hard-earned rewards of Long Creek Falls are well worth the effort.

You pass by the brink of the falls before the trail finally reaches the river's edge. Once at the river, head right and follow the river upstream a short distance until you reach Long Creek at its confluence with the Wild and Scenic Chattooga River. For the best views of the falls, cross Long Creek and follow it upstream to the base of Long Creek Falls.

Long Creek Falls creates the perfect picture as it flows over the rocks and converges with Section IV of the Chattooga River. If you want these falls to yourself, avoid getting here at lunchtime; whitewater rafters stop here for lunch daily. This is a popular landmark among the paddling community and a treat for all who visit.

The Chattooga River was also the setting of the 1972 Burt Reynolds–Ned Beatty film *Deliverance.* Some of its most famous scenes were filmed just over a mile downstream at Camp Creek.

FATHOM THIS

A fathom is a unit of measurement, length to be exact, equal to 6 feet. This nautical term is used to describe depth of water. So is the term *league,* as in *20,000 Leagues under the Sea.* A league is equal to three nautical miles. A nautical mile (a mile over sea) is not the same as a statute mile (a mile over land) and is actually 1.15 times longer than a statute mile. So, by these terms, the average depth of the Wild and Scenic Chattooga River ranges from less than 1 fathom to over 2 fathoms, and its length of 57 statute miles translates to just under 50 nautical miles.

Miles and Directions

0.0 From the trailhead, hike southwest down the bumpy forest roadbed.

0.1 Come to a fork in the road. Go right and continue hiking north-northwest.

0.6 The road leads you to a second fork with two old roadbeds. Go right (west) here as well, following the less-overgrown roadbed downhill. The roadbed soon narrows to a footpath.

0.7 Come to a sign for the WILD AND SCENIC CHATTOOGA RIVER. Continue hiking straight ahead (northwest) past the sign.

1.5 Reach an obvious side trail on the left (northwest) that heads down to the river. Follow this trail steeply down.

1.7 Pass the brink of the falls. Continue making your way west, steeply down toward the river.

1.8 Reach the edge of the Chattooga River. Go right, following the river north and upstream.

1.9 Come to Long Creek where the creek flows out into the river just downstream of the falls. For the best view, cross Long Creek and then follow it upstream a short distance to the base of Long Creek Falls (N34 47.131 / W83 19.382). Return the way you came.

3.8 Arrive back at the trailhead.

41 Brasstown Falls

Stellar! Shining like the stars and the heavens above, Brasstown Falls glimmers with excitement. Three incredible waterfalls greet you along this short but steep trail. If you're lucky, as I was, you might just catch a rainbow from the spray of Middle Falls. Brasstown Falls easily makes the Author's Favorites List, with all three falls earning a beauty rating of excellent.

Height: Upper Falls, 35 feet; Middle Falls, 25 feet; Lower Falls, 20 feet
Beauty rating: Excellent
Distance: 0.6 mile out and back
Difficulty: Moderate to strenuous
Trail surface: Hard-packed dirt
Approximate hiking time: 30 minutes
Blaze color: No blazes
County: Oconee

Land status: National forest
Trail contact: Sumter National Forest, Andrew Pickens Ranger District; (864) 638-9568; www.fs.fed.us
FYI: *Caution:* Not recommended for small children or dogs
Maps: *DeLorme: South Carolina Atlas & Gazetteer:* Page 16 C1; *DeLorme: Georgia Atlas & Gazetteer:* Page 16 E4

Finding the trailhead: From the junction of US 76 and US 441 in Clayton, Georgia, drive east on US 76 for 13.6 miles. Turn right onto Brasstown Road and travel 3.9 miles to a right turn onto FS 751 just before crossing the small bridge over Brasstown Creek. Follow FS 751 for 0.4 mile to where the road dead-ends. (**Note:** At 2.6 miles, Brasstown Road becomes a dirt road.)

From the junction of US 76 and the Chatooga River Bridge (Georgia–South Carolina state line), drive east on US 76 for 5.6 miles. Turn right onto Brasstown Road and follow the directions above.

From the junction of US 76 and US 123, drive west on US 76 for 11.6 miles. Turn left onto Brasstown Road and follow the directions above.

The trailhead is located at the southwest end of the parking area. GPS: N34 43.148/W83 18.107

The Hike

Follow the obvious trail southwest, as it crosses an open field and then heads back into the woods. Bypass the few side trails that lead to primitive campsites along the way. Instead stay on the wide main path, which leads to a large primitive campsite. Head right before entering the campsite and follow the creek downstream. You soon arrive at the brink of Upper Brasstown Falls. A steep trail follows the creek downstream to the base of Upper Brasstown Falls, also known as Brasstown Cascade.

▶ Brass is an alloy made by mixing copper with zinc. This gold-colored metal is highly malleable, making it easy to cast into a wide variety of shapes. This attribute, combined with its acoustic properties, makes brass an ideal material for musical instruments, primarily horns such as trumpets and tubas.

Upper Brasstown Falls is the first of three treasures waiting to be discovered along this trail.

Continue your downstream descent to Middle Brasstown Falls, also known as Brasstown Veil. After enjoying this amazing view, follow the steep trail downstream, making your final descent to the base of Lower Brasstown Falls, also known as Brasstown Sluice.

Please use caution along this trail! The banks along the creek are very steep, and until you reach the base of Lower Brasstown Falls, when you are at the base of one waterfall, you sit at the brink of the next.

The Brasstown Valley was first explored by the Cherokee, who called it *Itseyi*, meaning "place of fresh green." Years later, white settlers confused *Itseyi* with another Cherokee word, *v-tsai-yi,* meaning "brass." Soon after, the area known as "Brass-town" came to be.

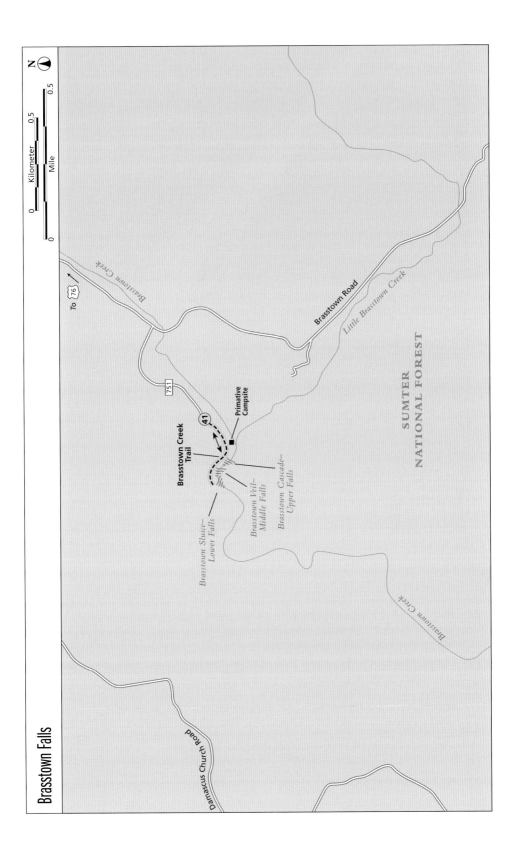

Brasstown Falls

N

Kilometer
0   0.5

Mile
0   0.5

To 76

Brasstown Creek

Brasstown Road

Little Brasstown Creek

751

41

Primative
Campsite

Brasstown Creek
Trail

Brasstown Sluice–
Lower Falls

Brasstown Veil–
Middle Falls

Brasstown Cascade–
Upper Falls

SUMTER
NATIONAL FOREST

Brasstown Creek

Damascus Church
Road

Lower Brasstown Falls, aka Brasstown Sluice, completes the threesome.

Miles and Directions

0.0 From the trailhead, hike southwest on the obvious trail as it crosses an open field and then leads back into the woods. Bypass the few side trails that lead to primitive campsites, and continue hiking on the wide path.

0.1 Come to a large primitive campsite. Head right (west) before entering the campsite, following Brasstown Creek downstream.

0.2 Arrive at the brink and then base of Upper Brasstown Falls (N34 43.118 / W83 18.253). Continue your descent as you hike north, following the creek downstream.

0.25 Arrive at the base of Middle Brasstown Falls (N34 43.129 / W83 18.265). Follow the steep trail north, and downstream, as you make your final descent.

0.3 Arrive at Lower Brasstown Falls (N34 43.129 / W83 18.316). Return the way you came.

0.6 Arrive back at the trailhead.

42 Chau Ram Falls

Sweet! This peaceful, stony-faced fall is located inside Chau Ram Park. A short walk from your vehicle takes you to the large, flat stones at the base of the falls. This is a great place for a picnic or to bring the little ones.

See overview map on page iv.
Height: 30 feet
Beauty rating: Very good
Distance: Roadside
Difficulty: Easy
Blaze color: No blazes
County: Oconee
Land status: County park
Trail contact: Oconee County Parks, Chau Ram

Park; (864) 888-1488; www.oconeecountry .com/chaurampark.html
FYI: Open 7 a.m. to dusk Mar to Nov 16; closed Martin Luther King Jr. Day, Thanksgiving, Christmas, New Year's Day; small fee
Maps: *DeLorme: South Carolina Atlas & Gazetteer:* Page 22 C2; *DeLorme: Georgia Atlas & Gazetteer:* Page 16 E5

Finding the trailhead: From the junction of US 76 and US 441 in Clayton, Georgia, drive east on US 76 for 22.8 miles. Turn right onto Chau Ram Park Road and follow it for 0.3 mile to the main entrance to the park. Continue for another 0.25 mile, going past the park office and around to the right to where the road dead-ends at a large parking lot.

From the junction of US 76 and the Chattooga River Bridge (Georgia–South Carolina state line), drive east on US 76 for 14.8 miles. Turn right onto Chau Ram Park Road and follow the directions above.

From the junction of US 76 and US 123, drive west on US 76 for 2.4 miles. Turn left onto Chau Ram Park Road and follow the directions above.

GPS: N34 40.929 / W83 08.710

The Hike

Chau Ram Falls can be viewed from the parking area as Ramsey Creek passes through the park on its way to the Chauga River.

In addition to the roadside Chau Ram Falls, Chau Ram Park has several hiking trails that offer great views of five other "falls" on the river. Actually they are rapids, including Can Opener and V rapids. Trail maps are available in the park office, and I definitely recommend exploring these trails while you are here.

Chau Ram Falls is perfect for everyone; you can drive right up to the base.

The trails can be reached by crossing the 175-foot-long pedestrian footbridge over the Chauga River, which makes for yet another unique experience while visiting the park.

43 Yellow Branch Falls

Three-dimensional! Absolutely surreal, Yellow Branch Falls is like a Mayan village up on a hillside, with its many facets seeming to come to life. The depth of this waterfall is unlike anything I've ever seen before. Definitely one of the most unusual waterfalls I've ever experienced, Yellow Branch Falls is my new favorite waterfall.

Height: 60 feet
Beauty rating: Excellent × 3
Distance: 3.0 miles out and back
Difficulty: Moderate to strenuous
Trail surface: Hard-packed dirt
Approximate hiking time: 1 hour, 30 minutes
Blaze color: No blazes
County: Oconee

Land status: National forest
Trail contact: Sumter National Forest, Andrew Pickens Ranger District; (864) 638-9568; www.fs.fed.us
Maps: *DeLorme: South Carolina Atlas & Gazetteer:* Page 22 A2; *DeLorme: Georgia Atlas & Gazetteer:* Page 16 D5

Finding the trailhead: From the junction of SC 28 and SC 107, drive south on SC 28 for 2.7 miles and turn right at the sign into the Yellow Branch Picnic Ground. Bypass a road that immediately heads up and to your right, and continue straight ahead for 0.2 mile to where the road dead-ends at a parking area.

From the junction of SC 28 and SC 183, drive north on SC 28 for 5.3 miles. Turn left at the sign into the Yellow Branch Picnic Ground and follow the directions above.

The trailhead is accessed from the southwest side of the parking lot. GPS: N34 48.335 / W83 07.731

The Hike

A short path on the southwest side of the parking lot takes you west-southwest to a large trail information sign and the trailhead. The trail follows a tiny brook downstream as it makes its way into the thickness of the forest before leading you to a small stream. Rock-hop across, and continue hiking as you rock-hop two more small creeks. Shortly after rock-hopping the third small creek, where the trail begins to bend left (northeast) you will see a side trail on the right (south) with a set of steps that head down to a wooden footbridge. (There should be a marker on a tree reading FALLS at this side trail.) Go down the steps and cross the footbridge.

Continue to follow the obvious trail as it takes you along the forest floor. After a short distance, the trail forks at yet another creek. Go left here, cross the creek, and pick the trail up on the other side. The now easy-to-follow trail heads southeast and leads you away from the creek. Although you can't hear any water, trust me; patience pays with this one.

The indescribable Yellow Branch Falls is a must-see.

The trail continues through the forest as it makes a slow descent and crosses another wooden footbridge. A short distance after this footbridge, the trail narrows and forks up and to the right (south). Follow this right fork as it takes you around (west) and crosses another footbridge.

Continue hiking southeast as the trail begins to climb and circle the mountainside. As the trail begins to head back downhill, you'll hear the encouraging sounds of water. Remember . . . patience. This is not your waterfall. Continue north on the main trail, again moving away from the sounds of the water. Soon the sounds of your destination come into range and you begin the final descent to the base of the three-dimensional Yellow Branch Falls.

The Yellow Branch Picnic Ground has been around since at least the 1930s, with one of the original buildings still standing today. Oconee County, within which the picnic ground is located, has been around for hundreds of years longer. Many stories exist about how the county came to be named, most of which stem from Native American roots. The theory I prefer is that it takes its name from the Cherokee word *Uk-oo-na,* meaning "watery eyes of the hills." Take a peek at the abundance of creeks, lakes, and waterfalls around here and you'll understand why I prefer this one.

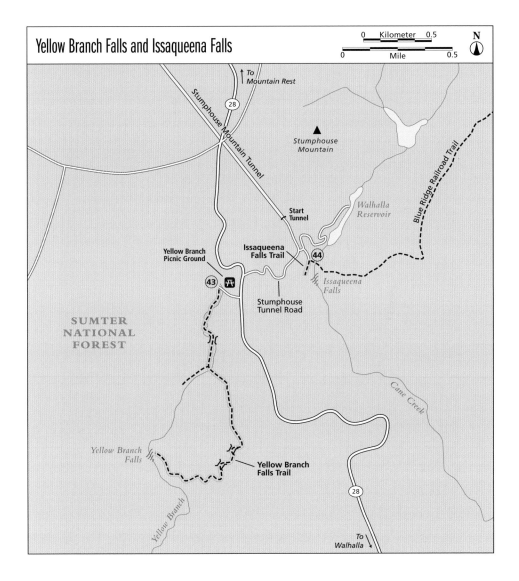

Yellow Branch Falls and Issaqueena Falls

0   Kilometer   0.5

0   Mile   0.5

N

To Mountain Rest

28

▲ Stumphouse Mountain

Stumphouse Mountain Tunnel

Start Tunnel

Walhalla Reservoir

Blue Ridge Railroad Trail

Yellow Branch Picnic Ground

Issaqueena Falls Trail

44

43

Issaqueena Falls

Stumphouse Tunnel Road

SUMTER NATIONAL FOREST

Cane Creek

Yellow Branch Falls

Yellow Branch Falls Trail

28

Yellow Branch

To Walhalla

Miles and Directions

0.0   From the trailhead, hike southeast, following the tiny stream downstream and into the forest. Rock-hop across the trickling stream and continue southeast. Rock-hop two more small streams and continue hiking south.

0.3   Come to a side trail on the right (south) with a marker on a tree reading FALLS and some steps that head down to a footbridge. Head down the steps and cross the footbridge. Continue hiking south on the obvious trail as it takes you along the forest floor.

0.5   Come to a fork where the trail reaches the creek. Go left (east) here, cross the creek, and pick the trail up on the other side. From here the trail heads southeast and away from the creek.

Dogs are allowed on most trails, but make sure you keep them on a leash, for everyone's sake.

1.0 Cross another wooden footbridge. A short distance after the crossing, the trail narrows and forks up to the right (south). Follow this right fork as the trail takes you around to the west.

1.1 Cross another footbridge and continue hiking southeast as the trail begins to climb and circle the mountainside.

1.5 Arrive at the base of Yellow Branch Falls (N34 47.701 / W83 08.025). Return the way you came.

3.0 Arrive back at the trailhead.

44 Issaqueena Falls

Captivating! The way nature comes together here shows the unity of all living things needing one another to survive. The ecosystem that creates this waterfall is fantastic.

See map on page 147.
Height: 100 feet
Beauty rating: Excellent
Distance: 0.2 mile out and back
Difficulty: Easy
Trail surface: Wide mulch path
Approximate hiking time: 10 minutes
Blaze color: No blazes
County: Oconee

Land status: National forest
Trail contact: Sumter National Forest, Andrew Pickens Ranger District; (864) 638-9568; www.fs.fed.us
FYI: Park hours vary through the year
Maps: DeLorme: South Carolina Atlas & Gazetteer: Page 22 A2; DeLorme: Georgia Atlas & Gazetteer: Page 16 D5

Finding the trailhead: From the junction of SC 28 and SC 107, drive south on SC 28 for 2.6 miles. Turn left onto Stumphouse Tunnel Road at the sign for Stumphouse Tunnel Park and drive down the hill for 0.5 mile. At the bottom of the hill, turn right onto the narrow side road and immediately go right again, heading to the picnic area.

From the junction of SC 28 and SC 183, drive north on SC 28 for 5.4 miles. Turn right onto Stumphouse Tunnel Road at the sign for Stumphouse Tunnel Park and follow the directions above.

The trailhead is located to the right of the information signpost at the south end of the parking area. GPS: N34 48.449 / W83 07.285

The Hike

Issaqueena Falls is located within Stumphouse Tunnel Park. The information signpost at the trailhead tells the tale of the Indian maiden for whom the falls were named.

Hike south a short distance and cross the wooden bridge as you make your way toward the sound of the falls. As you continue to follow the wide mulch path, you will come to and cross a second covered wooden bridge. The path leads downhill a short distance farther to an observation deck overlooking Issaqueena Falls.

Issaqueena was an Indian maiden who fell in love with a white settler. Her lover was David Francis, a silversmith who lived in what is now the town of Ninety-six, South Carolina. Upon hearing that her tribe was planning to attack his town, Issaqueena rode on horseback some 92 miles to warn the settlers of the pending attack.

The settlers escaped, and David and Issaqueena fled to Stumphouse Mountain, where they lived in a hollowed out tree or "stump house." When her tribe finally tracked them down, Issaqueena fled to the falls, where she leapt from the brink. The tribesmen thought her to be dead and gave up the chase, but she had landed in a small cave behind the falls. Hidden by the veil of water, she stayed there for days before rejoining her husband. The pair then fled to Alabama and lived happily ever after.

Clemson College once cured its famous blue cheese deep inside the Stumphouse Mountain Tunnel.

For an interesting side trip, visit the Stumphouse Mountain Tunnel. To get there, continue another 0.1 mile on Stumphouse Tunnel Road to where the road dead-ends at a parking area. From the parking area, head northeast up the hill to the entrance of this 1,600-foot-deep tunnel.

THE CURE FOR BLUE CHEESE

Clemson College purchased the Stumphouse Tunnel in 1951 because of its constant temperature and high humidity. Why, one might ask? To cure blue cheese of course.

A professor in Clemson College's Dairy department realized that the tunnel had the perfect climate to cure cheese. The college began in-depth studies, and the next thing you know, they were making the cheese on campus and then transporting it to the Stumphouse Mountain Tunnel for curing. This project continued with great success from 1951 until 1958, when the college was able to duplicate the tunnel's climate and began curing the cheese in special labs on campus called "cheese rooms."

Clemson University still uses the same ripening recipe for curing its world-famous blue cheese that it did back in the early 1950s in the Stumphouse Mountain Tunnel.

Miles and Directions

0.0 From the trailhead, hike south on the wide mulch path. Cross the wooden bridge and make your way toward the sound of the falls. Cross a second covered footbridge and continue downhill.

0.1 Arrive at the overlook for Issaqueena Falls (N34 48.390 / W83 07.308). Return the way you came.

0.2 Arrive back at the trailhead.

45 Cedar Creek Falls

Symbiotic! As the waters of Cedar Creek flow past, I can't help but ponder the complex, yet simple, ways of nature. The amazing link among all living things within an ecosystem always leaves me in awe.

Height: 20 feet
Beauty rating: Good
Distance: 1.2 miles out and back
Difficulty: Easy to moderate; steep scramble to the base
Trail surface: Wide forest road
Approximate hiking time: 40 minutes
Blaze color: No blazes

County: Oconee
Land status: National forest
Trail contact: Sumter National Forest, Andrew Pickens Ranger District; (864) 638-9568; www.fs.fed.us
Maps: *DeLorme: South Carolina Atlas & Gazetteer:* Page 22 A2; *DeLorme: Georgia Atlas & Gazetteer:* Page 16 D5

Finding the trailhead: From the junction of SC 28 and SC 107, drive south on SC 28 for 1.9 miles. Turn right onto Whetstone Road and travel 0.7 mile to a left turn onto Cassidy Bridge Road. Continue for 0.85 mile before turning left onto the gravel FS 744 (Rich Mountain Road). Travel 3.2 miles and turn right onto FS 744C. Continue for 2.5 miles to FS 2658 on your right. Park here, but don't block the gate.

From the junction of SC 28 and SC 183, drive north on SC 28 for 6.1 miles. Turn left onto Whetstone Road and follow the directions above.

GPS: N34 45.706/W83 11.161

The Hike

Begin by hiking down the gated FS 2658. After approximately 0.25 mile on the forest service road, the road bends to the left and you will see two stone-blocked roads shooting off to the right. The first road is before the bend and heads down; the second is after the bend and goes up. You want to take the first.

Go around the boulders and follow the wide path alongside the creek. The wide path bends to the left (north) and then reaches a fork at the creek. Go left (southwest) at the fork and down, and soon find yourself alongside Cedar Creek Falls.

Several side trails make their way steeply down to the base. Choose your path, but use caution! The way to the base is extremely steep, and once you arrive at the base of Cedar Creek Falls, you are also at the brink of Blue Hole Falls. (**Note:** Although Blue Hole Falls is just a stone's throw away, I have not included it in this guide because there is no safe way to reach it.)

Cedar Creek Falls

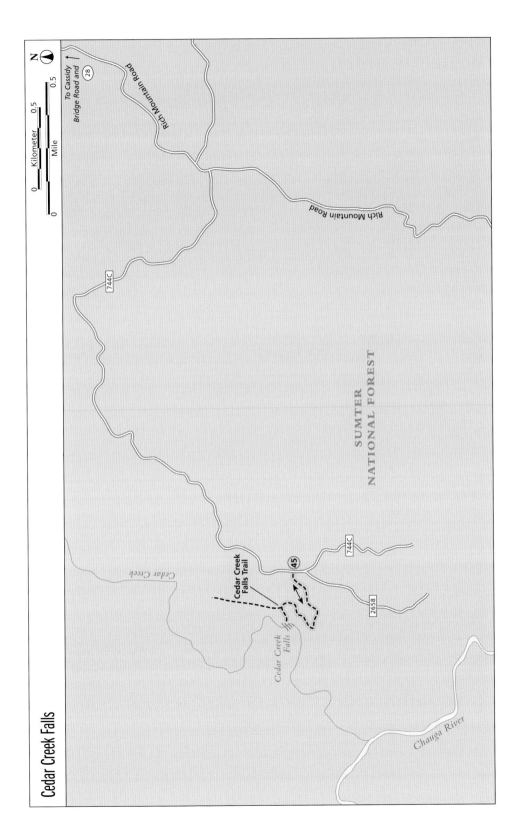

Cedar Creek Falls is a perfect place to relax on the rocks and soak in the sun's rays.

Cedar Creek is one of the many feeder creeks to the Chauga River. The nearby Cassidy Bridge Campground offers primitive camping and is very popular among hunters during season. Between the campground and the National Forest Service Rifle Range off Cassidy Bridge Road, don't be surprised if you hear gunshots while visiting this waterfall.

Miles and Directions

0.0 From the parking area, hike north-northwest down the gated FS 2658.

0.25 Where FS 2658 bends to the left, two stone-blocked roads shoot off to the right. Take the road before the bend which heads downhill (northeast). Go around the boulders and follow this wide path alongside the creek.

0.5 Arrive at the creek and a fork, with the main trail heading right (northwest) and down and a side trail heading left (southwest) and down. Take the trail to the left and soon arrive alongside Cedar Creek Falls. Carefully follow one of several steep trails down to the base.

0.6 Arrive at the base of Cedar Creek Falls (N34 45.727 / W83 11.374). Return the way you came.

1.2 Arrive back at the trailhead.

46 Chauga Narrows

Tremendous! Chauga Narrows flows like freedom itself, carving its way through the bonds of the boulders and then dropping to the calm of the river below. This one makes you feel as though you've entered another world, where nature rules and man is subservient to its will.

Height: 25 feet
Beauty rating: Excellent
Distance: 1.2 miles out and back
Difficulty: Brink, easy to moderate; base, strenuous
Trail surface: Hard-packed dirt
Approximate hiking time: 50 minutes
Blaze color: No blazes

County: Oconee
Land status: National forest
Trail contact: Sumter National Forest, Andrew Pickens Ranger District; (864) 638-9568; www.fs.fed.us
Maps: *DeLorme: South Carolina Atlas & Gazetteer:* Page 16 H2; *DeLorme: Georgia Atlas & Gazetteer:* Page 16 C5

Finding the trailhead: From the junction of US 76 and US 441 in Clayton, Georgia, drive east on US 76 for 10.0 miles. Turn left onto Chattooga Ridge Road and travel 5.7 miles to a four-way stop sign at Whetstone Road. Go right here, following Whetstone Road for 1.0 mile to a pull-off on the left just before the road crosses the Chauga River Bridge.

From the junction of US 76 and the Chattooga River Bridge (Georgia–South Carolina state line), drive east on US 76 for 2.0 miles. Turn left onto Chattooga Ridge Road and follow the directions above.

From the junction of US 76 and SC 123, drive west on US 76 for 15.2 miles. Turn right onto Chattooga Ridge Road and follow the directions above.

From the junction of SC 28 and SC 107, drive south on SC 28 for 1.9 miles. Turn right onto Whetstone Road and travel 5.0 miles to a pull-off on the right just after the road crosses the Chauga River Bridge.

The trailhead is located on the opposite (south) side of the road from the pull-off. GPS: N34 50.021 / W83 10.533

The Hike

Cross the street from the pull-off and hike a short distance down the dirt road toward the river. As you near the river, you will see the remains of an old bridge over the Chauga River. From here the road bends right, heads into the woods, and parallels the river downstream. After you hike on the old logging road for approximately 0.25 mile, the logging road transforms into a narrow, overgrown path.

Continue along the narrow footpath, still following the river downstream. You pass some small rapids and then through a rhododendron tunnel. From here the trail makes a hard bend to the right and leads past a primitive campsite. You soon hear the

The Chauga River roars through Chauga Narrows.

fury of the rapids downstream, and the trail seems to end. Head steeply up to your right to pick up the path again.

Continue following the river downstream and arrive at the middle section of Chauga Narrows. The trail continues steeply downstream until the river calms just beyond the rapid. A side trail to the left leads even more steeply down to the river's edge to the base of Chauga Narrows.

Chauga is Cherokee for "high and lifted up stream." It seems, however, that the river is just the opposite as it drops an average of 60 to 80 feet per mile on the way to its confluence with the Savannah River. A 9.8-mile stretch of the Chauga is very popular with whitewater rafters. They say its Class I through V rapids easily rival those on the famed Wild and Scenic Chattooga River.

Miles and Directions

0.0 From the trailhead, hike southeast on the old logging road as it heads down toward the river. The road takes you past the remains of an old bridge over the river and then bends to the right (south) as it leads back into the woods and follows the river downstream.

0.25 The old logging road becomes a narrow, overgrown path as you hike southeast along the river's edge.

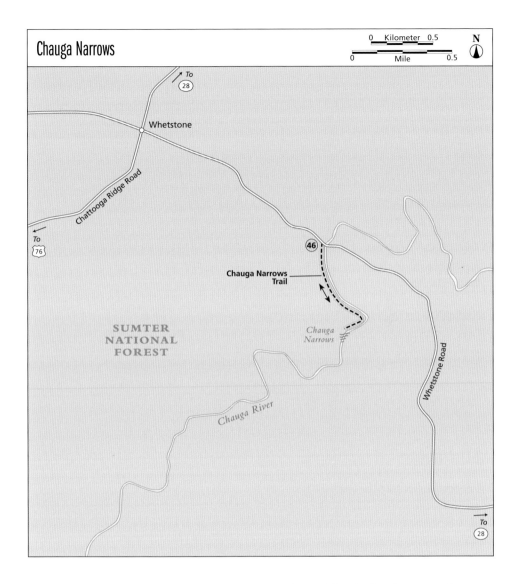

Chauga Narrows

0   Kilometer 0.5

0   Mile   0.5

N

To
(28)

Whetstone

Chattooga Ridge Road

To
(76)

(46)

Chauga Narrows
Trail

SUMTER
NATIONAL
FOREST

Chauga
Narrows

Whetstone Road

Chauga River

To
(28)

0.4 Pass through a rhododendron tunnel as you continue to follow the river downstream. As the river bends to the right (southwest), you pass by a primitive campsite.

0.5 The trail seems to end as you hear the fury of the rapids downstream. Head steeply up to the right (northwest) to pick up the path again.

0.6 Reach Chauga Narrows (N34 49.620 / W83 10.393). Return the way you came.

1.2 Arrive back at the trailhead.

47 Pigpen and Licklog Falls

Ideal! This trail gives you two great waterfalls back to back. With a perfect camping area at Pigpen Falls and a fabulous flow straight out into the Wild and Scenic Chattooga River, Licklog Falls is yet another treat to be found along this amazing river.

Height: Pigpen Falls, 10 feet; Licklog Falls, 25 feet
Beauty rating: Very good
Distance: Licklog Falls, 2.2 miles out and back (Pigpen Falls, 1.4 miles)
Difficulty: Easy to moderate
Trail surface: Hard-packed dirt
Approximate hiking time: 1 hour, 10 minutes
Blaze color: White

County: Oconee
Land status: National forest
Trail contact: Sumter National Forest, Andrew Pickens Ranger District; (864) 638-9568; www.fs.fed.us
Maps: *DeLorme: South Carolina Atlas & Gazetteer:* Page 16 G2; *DeLorme: Georgia Atlas & Gazetteer:* Page 16 B5

Finding the trailhead: From the junction of SC 107 and SC 28, drive north on SC 107 for 3.3 miles. Turn left onto Village Creek Road and travel 1.7 miles to a right turn onto Nicholson Ford Road just before the road makes a hard bend to the left (east). Follow Nicholson Ford Road for 2.2 miles to where it dead-ends. (**Note:** Along the way, Nicholson Ford Road becomes FS 2603.)
From the junction of SC 107 and SC 413 (Wiggington Road), drive south on SC 107 for 10.5 miles. Turn right onto Village Creek Road and follow the directions above.
GPS: N34 55.509 / W83 07.341

The Hike

The trail begins at the northeast end of the parking area by the trail information signpost. (Ignore the trail up the steps on the right or southeast side.) Head straight back (northeast) into the woods, following the white blazes. A wide variety of birdlife call this area home. Their songs serenade you before the sound of the creek drowns them out.

As you enjoy your surroundings, the trail makes a slow and steady descent until you arrive at a primitive campsite next to a creek. Pass the campsite and you soon come to a wooden footbridge over the creek. Cross the bridge and reach another primitive campsite. Continue straight ahead (west-southwest); the trail crosses another wooden footbridge. Pick up the easily followed trail on the other side as it follows the creek downstream.

Pass a small cascade on the left, head down the hill, and come to a fork at a sign reading CHATTOOGA S. Go left (southwest) at this fork, following the trail downhill to a footbridge over the creek at the base of Pigpen Falls. This is a great place to have a creekside picnic or just sit a spell.

This peaceful portion of the Chattooga River sits at the base of Licklog Falls.

After basking in the beauty of Pigpen Falls, cross the bridge and head to the right, following the creek downstream. After hiking less than 0.25 mile you arrive at the brink of Licklog Falls. Continue downstream a bit farther. As the trail bends left (west), you will see an obvious side trail on the right (north-northeast) that leads you on a steep and strenuous scramble down to the river. Take this side trail all the way down to the river to get a view of Licklog Falls from the base.

Licklog Creek flows into Section 0 on the headwaters portion of the Wild and Scenic Chattooga River. The crown jewel of the Southern rivers, the Chattooga is most famous for its whitewater rafting but can also be appreciated from land. The Chattooga River Trail, which can be accessed here, is a fabulous 40-mile-long foot trail that follows the banks of the river and borders both South Carolina and Georgia.

Miles and Directions

0.0 From the trailhead, hike northeast, following the white blazes straight back into the woods. The trail makes a slow and steady descent.

0.5 Pass a primitive campsite next to a creek and continue hiking northwest to a wooden footbridge over the creek. Cross the bridge and come to another primitive campsite. Continue hiking straight ahead (west-southwest).

0.6 Cross another wooden footbridge and pick up the easily followed trail on the other side. As you follow the creek downstream and west, pass a small cascade on the left and continue down the hill.

Pigpen Falls and Licklog Falls

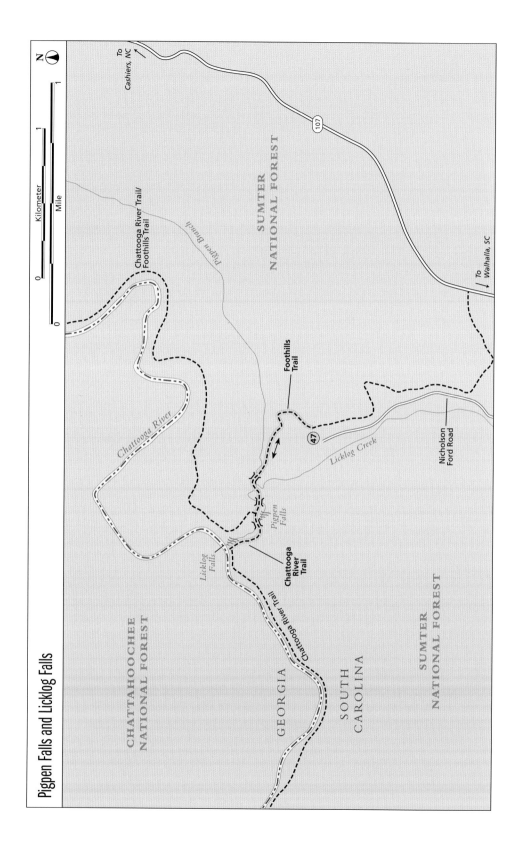

N

Kilometer

Mile

To
Cashiers, NC

107

SUMTER
NATIONAL FOREST

To
Walhalla, SC

Chattooga River Trail/
Foothills Trail

Pigpen Branch

Foothills
Trail

Chattooga River

47

Licklog Creek

Nicholson
Ford Road

Licklog
Falls

Pigpen
Falls

Chattooga
River Trail

Chattooga River Trail

CHATTAHOOCHEE
NATIONAL FOREST

GEORGIA

SOUTH
CAROLINA

SUMTER
NATIONAL FOREST

Ursus americanus, the American black bear, is unique to North America and roams throughout the mountains of Georgia and South Carolina.

0.7 Reach a fork at a sign reading Cʜᴀᴛᴛᴏᴏɢᴀ S. Go left (southwest) at the fork and follow the trail down to another footbridge over the creek at the base of Pigpen Falls (N34 55.715/W83 07.749). (*Option:* Turn around and return to the trailhead for a 1.4-mile hike of about 45 minutes.) After enjoying Pigpen Falls, cross the bridge and head right (west), following Licklog Creek downstream.

0.9 Arrive at the brink of Licklog Falls. Continue to follow the creek downstream.

1.0 As the trail begins to bend to the left (west), an obvious side trail on the right leads you north-northeast on a steep and strenuous scramble down to the river.

1.1 Arrive at the base of Licklog Falls, where Licklog Creek meets the mighty Chattooga River (N34 55.821/W83 07.864). Return the way you came.

2.2 Arrive back at the trailhead.

48 King Creek Falls

Proud! King Creek Falls stands proudly above the creek it feeds, like a fledgling taking its first flight and shouting, "Hey, look at me!"

Height: 60 feet
Beauty rating: Excellent
Distance: 1.4 miles out and back
Difficulty: Easy to moderate
Trail surface: Hard-packed dirt
Approximate hiking time: 40 minutes
Blaze color: White
County: Oconee

Land status: National forest
Trail contact: Sumter National Forest, Andrew Pickens Ranger District; (864) 638-9568; www.fs.fed.us
Maps: *DeLorme: South Carolina Atlas & Gazetteer:* Page 16 F2-F3; *DeLorme: Georgia Atlas & Gazetteer:* Page 16 A5, 17 A6

Finding the trailhead: From the junction of SC 107 and SC 28, drive north on SC 107 for 10.0 miles. Turn left onto New Burrell's Ford Road and travel 2.2 miles to a left turn into the parking area for Burrell's Ford Campground.

From the junction of SC 107 and SC 413 (Wiggington Road), drive south on SR 107 for 3.8 miles. Turn right onto New Burrell's Ford Road at the sign for BURRELL'S FORD and follow the directions above.

The trailhead is located at the southwest corner of the parking area at the trail information signpost. GPS: N34 58.271 / W83 06.888

The Hike

The trail begins just behind the signpost and heads south back into the woods. Follow the narrow, white-blazed path as it winds down into the forest. Just before reaching the creek, you come to an intersection with another trail. Go straight ahead here and cross the wooden footbridge in front of you.

After crossing the bridge, head left (southeast) and follow the creek upstream. You soon arrive at a fork in the trail, with steps going up to your left and the Foothills Trail heading right. Go left here, heading up the steps and continuing upstream. Pass the wonderful cascades along the way as you continue hiking until the trail ends at the base of King Creek Falls.

The trail and surrounding area are best known for their splendid diversity of birdlife. The altitude is around 2,800 feet, yet bird species typical of elevations up to 4,000 feet are commonly found here. You may want to bring some binoculars and do some birding on your way to the falls.

Burrell's Ford Campground offers primitive camping only; there are no facilities available.

Canyoneers rappel down the face of King Creek Falls.

Miles and Directions

0.0   From the trailhead, hike south into the woods on the narrow, white-blazed trail as it winds down into the forest.

0.4   Just before reaching the creek, come to an intersection with a trail that heads northwest and follows the creek downstream. Ignore this trail and instead go straight ahead (south), continuing to follow the Foothills Trail over a wooden footbridge. After crossing the footbridge, head left (southeast) and follow the creek upstream.

King Creek Falls and Spoon Auger Falls

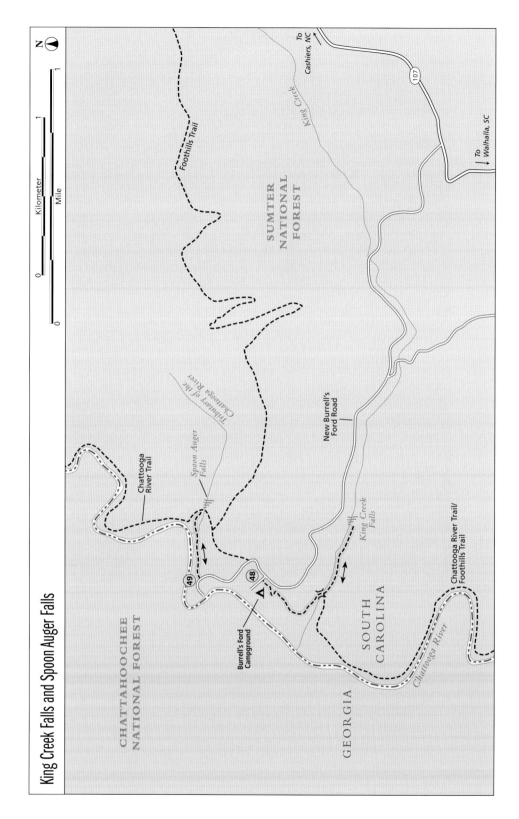

N

0   Kilometer   1

0   Mile   1

CHATTAHOOCHEE
NATIONAL FOREST

SUMTER
NATIONAL
FOREST

GEORGIA

SOUTH
CAROLINA

Foothills Trail

Chattooga River Trail

Spoon Auger Falls

Tributary of the
Chattooga River

Burrell's Ford
Campground

49

48

New Burrell's
Ford Road

King Creek
Falls

King Creek

Chattooga River

Chattooga River Trail/
Foothills Trail

To
Cashiers, NC

107

To
Walhalla, SC

CANYONEERING

Canyoneering is a sport that entails traveling through canyons and often following the creeks and rivers that run through them. So what makes this different from hiking?

Canyoneers actually hike down the creek or river itself, not alongside it. Whether jumping from rock to rock, trudging through chilling water, or rappelling down the face of a waterfall, these brave explorers use whatever means of travel necessary. It's quite common to see them with climbing harnesses, rope bags, and even a wet suit as they make their way through the icy mountain waters around us.

0.5 Arrive at a fork in the trail with some steps going up and to the left (east) and the Foothills Trail heading the right (west). Go left, head up the steps, and continue following the creek upstream.

0.7 The trail ends at the base of King Creek Falls (N34 57.981 / W83 06.650). Return the way you came.

1.4 Arrive back at the trailhead.

49 Spoon Auger Falls

Happy! Spoon Auger Falls smiles at you, as the sprinkles fly from her face, to cool and refresh you, in perfect tiny droplets.

See map on page 164.
Height: 100 feet
Beauty rating: Good
Distance: 0.6 mile out and back
Difficulty: Moderate
Trail surface: Hard-packed dirt
Approximate hiking time: 25 minutes
Blaze color: No blazes

County: Oconee
Land status: National forest
Trail contact: Sumter National Forest, Andrew Pickens Ranger District; (864) 638-9568; www.fs.fed.us
Maps: *DeLorme: South Carolina Atlas & Gazetteer:* Page 16 F2-F3; *DeLorme: Georgia Atlas & Gazetteer:* Page 16 A5, 17 A6

Finding the trailhead: From the junction of SC 107 and SC 28, drive north on SC 107 for 10.0 miles. Turn left onto New Burrell's Ford Road at the sign for BURRELL'S FORD and travel 2.55 miles to a pull-off along the right side of the road next to the trail information sign.

From the junction of SC 107 and SC 413 (Wiggington Road), drive south on SC 107 for 3.8 miles. Turn right onto New Burrell's Ford Road at the sign for BURRELL'S FORD and follow the directions above.

The trailhead is located on the north side of the parking area next to the trail information sign. GPS: N34 58.491/W83 06.884

The Hike

Hike east as the trail leads straight back into the woods. Bypass any small side paths, staying on the wide main trail as it follows the Chattooga River upstream. You will rock- or log-hop across two small tributaries before reaching the creek. Rock-hop across this as well.

As soon as you cross the creek, the trail leads upstream for a short distance back to the creek and then makes a sharp switchback to the left. Follow this switchback and begin climbing uphill. You make three more switchbacks before the trail straightens out and dead-ends at the base of Spoon Auger Falls.

Spoon Auger is located at the far south end of the Ellicott Rock Wilderness. Named for Andrew Ellicott, who surveyed the North Carolina–South Carolina borders around 1811, the wilderness covers 8,274 acres within North Carolina, South Carolina, and Georgia.

In the center of it all, lying on the east bank of the Chattooga River is the famed Ellicott Rock. Andrew Ellicott chiseled an inconspicuous mark on this boulder to denote the junction of all three states. To this day, the rock marks the spot. Ellicott Rock was placed on the National Registry of Historical Places in 1973.

You can camp right along the banks of Lake Keowee at High Falls Park, but don't be fooled—there is no High Falls here.

Miles and Directions

0.0 From the trailhead, the trail heads east, straight back into the woods. Bypass any small side paths and stay on the wide trail as it follows the Chattooga River upstream. Rock- or log-hop across two small tributaries and continue hiking east.

0.2 Arrive at the creek and rock-hop across. Go right (southeast) and head upstream for a short distance to the creek again. The trail makes a sharp switchback to the left (northeast). Follow this switchback and begin an uphill climb.

0.3 Arrive at the base of Spoon Auger Falls (N34 58.491 / W83 06.613). Return the way you came.

0.6 Arrive back at the trailhead.

50 Upper Sloan Bridge Falls, Lower Sloan Bridge Falls, and Hiker's Peril

Fresh! As you make your way alongside the river, the cool and fresh waters beside you fill your heart with joy, enticing you to immerse yourself within them. One refreshing treat after another awaits you on this short, yet enjoyable, section of the famed Foothills Trail.

Height: Upper Sloan Bridge Falls, 45 feet; Lower Sloan Bridge Falls, 10 feet; Hiker's Peril, 100+ feet

Beauty rating: Upper Sloan Bridge, very good; Lower Sloan Bridge, good; Hiker's Peril, fair

Distance: 1.4 miles out and back

Difficulty: Mostly easy, with a steep and strenuous scramble

Trail surface: Hard-packed dirt

Approximate hiking time: 1 hour

Blaze color: White

County: Oconee

Land status: National forest

Trail contact: Sumter National Forest, Andrew Pickens Ranger District; (864) 638-9568; www.fs.fed.us

FYI: Trash cans, small restroom, trail information sign at parking area

Maps: DeLorme: South Carolina Atlas & Gazetteer: Page 16 E3; DeLorme: Georgia Atlas & Gazetteer: Page 17 A6; DeLorme: North Carolina Atlas & Gazetteer: Page 52 F2

Finding the trailhead: From the junction of SC 107 and the North Carolina–South Carolina state line, drive south on SC 107 for 0.6 mile. Turn right into the unmarked paved parking area for Sloan Bridge Picnic Area.

From the junction of SC 107 and SC 413 (Wiggington Road), drive north on SC 107 for 0.15 mile. Turn left into the unmarked paved parking area for Sloan Bridge Picnic Area.

From the junction of SC 107 and SC 28, drive north on SC 107 for 14.0 miles. Turn left into the unmarked paved parking area for Sloan Bridge Picnic Area.

The trailhead is to the left, at the south end of the parking lot. GPS: N35 00.208 / W83 03.253

The Hike

From the trailhead the trail follows a portion of the white-blazed Foothills Trail. You immediately cross a small wooden bridge before coming to a trail information sign. Continue to follow the white blazes as the trail comes to and leaves the river from high above. After approximately 0.4 mile on the Foothills Trail, you arrive alongside the lively, three-tiered Upper Sloan Bridge Falls. A side path leads steeply to the base of the falls. This side trail is extremely steep and slippery—*please use caution!* Or, simply enjoy the view from the Foothills Trail.

From Upper Sloan Bridge Falls continue downstream for another 0.1 mile and get a good glimpse of Lower Sloan Bridge Falls from the trail above. Continue following

Upper Sloan Bridge Falls, Lower Sloan Bridge Falls, and Hiker's Peril

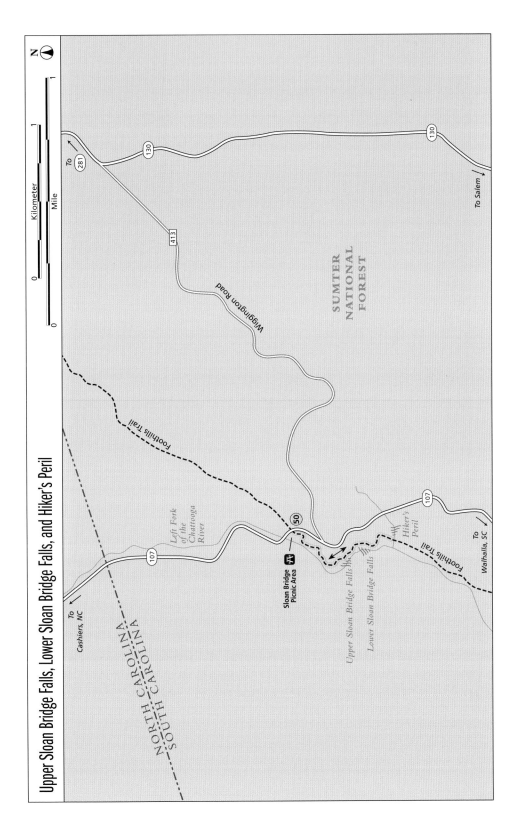

A burl such as this may indicate that the tree underwent some sort of stress.

the Foothills Trail for another 0.2 mile and arrive at a wooden footbridge over a portion of trail that is known as Hiker's Peril. Although the hike along the river is pleasant, Hiker's Peril itself is not a particularly attractive waterfall. As an option, you may consider skipping it and simply returning to the trailhead after viewing Lower Sloan Bridge Falls.

The banks of the river are so overgrown during spring and summer that viewing the falls from the Foothills Trail can be difficult during these seasons. I recommend hiking this one in wintertime, when the Upper and Lower Sloan Bridge Falls can be clearly viewed from the trail without having to scramble to the base.

This section of the 77-mile Foothills Trail is shared with the Fork Mountain Trail, which starts at streamside and makes its way to the top of Fork Mountain. At 3,294 feet, Fork Mountain is the tallest peak within the South Carolina tract of the Ellicott Wilderness and the second-highest summit in South Carolina.

▷ **The Foothills Trail stretches nearly 80 miles through upstate South Carolina and western North Carolina. This fabulous footpath leads past pristine preserves and wonderful waterfalls. As you make your way from the low country to the heights of Sassafras Mountain, a wealth of diversity awaits you.**

Miles and Directions

0.0 From the trailhead, hike south and immediately cross a small wooden bridge leading to a trail information sign. Continue to follow the white blazes as the trail comes to and leaves the river from high above.

0.4 Arrive alongside lively, three-tiered Upper Sloan Bridge Falls (N35 00.016 / W83 03.360). A side path leads west, steeply down to the base. From Upper Sloan Bridge, continue following the river downstream and south.

0.5 Arrive at Lower Sloan Bridge Falls (N34 59.942 / W83 03.306). You should be able to get a good glimpse of this one from the trail. Continue hiking south along the river.

0.7 Arrive at the small bridge over Hiker's Peril (N34 59.841 / W83 03.281). Return the way you came.

1.4 Arrive back at the trailhead.

Options: To shorten this hike to 1.0 mile round-trip, you may opt to turn around at 0.5 mile after enjoying both the Upper and Lower Sloan Bridge Falls.

51 Station Cove Falls

Unity! The water here flows over each little section, working together to create the creek, all the while feeding the moss and plants upon it.

Height: 80 feet
Beauty rating: Very good
Distance: 1.6 miles out and back
Difficulty: Easy
Trail surface: Hard-packed dirt
Approximate hiking time: 45 minutes
Blaze color: No blazes
County: Oconee
Land status: National Forest and State Historic Site

Trail contact: Sumter National Forest, Andrew Pickens Ranger District; (864) 638-9568; www.fs.fed.us
  Oconee Station State Historic Site; (864) 638-0079; www.southcarolinaparks.com
FYI: Oconee Station House is open to the public weekends 1 to 5 p.m.
Maps: *DeLorme: South Carolina Atlas & Gazetteer:* Page 16 H3; *DeLorme: Georgia Atlas & Gazetteer:* Page 17 C6

Finding the trailhead: From the junction of SC 11 and SC 183, drive north on SC 11 for 1.9 miles to where Oconee Station Road forks off to the left at the sign for Historical Oconee Station. Go left here and continue for 2.2 miles to a small parking area on the left at a trail information sign and just 0.1 mile past the entrance to the Oconee Station.

From the junction of SC 11 and SC 130, drive south on SC 11 for 6.6 miles. Turn right onto Oconee Station Road and follow the directions above.

The trailhead is located west of the parking area next to the trail information sign. GPS: N34 50.935/W83 04.470

The Hike

The wide trail heads straight back into the woods. Bypass any small side trails, staying on the wide main path as it takes you to a wooden footbridge. Cross the bridge and continue along the easily followed path as it meanders through the forest. You cross three more footbridges and come to a fork immediately after crossing the fourth footbridge. The right fork leads northwest 2.7 miles to Oconee State Park. The left fork heads west toward the falls. Go left here, and although you can't hear the sounds of any water, don't be discouraged.

Continue on the main trail until you reach the creek. Instead of crossing the creek, turn right and follow the creek upstream and slightly uphill. When Station Cove Falls comes into view in the distance, you see a set of stone steps leading down to the creek. Take the steps, cross the creek on the rocky "bridge," and then make your way upstream to the base of Station Cove Falls.

Located near the Oconee Station State Historic Site, Station Cove Falls was named for the historic Station House. Built in 1792, the Station House is the oldest

Station Cove Falls

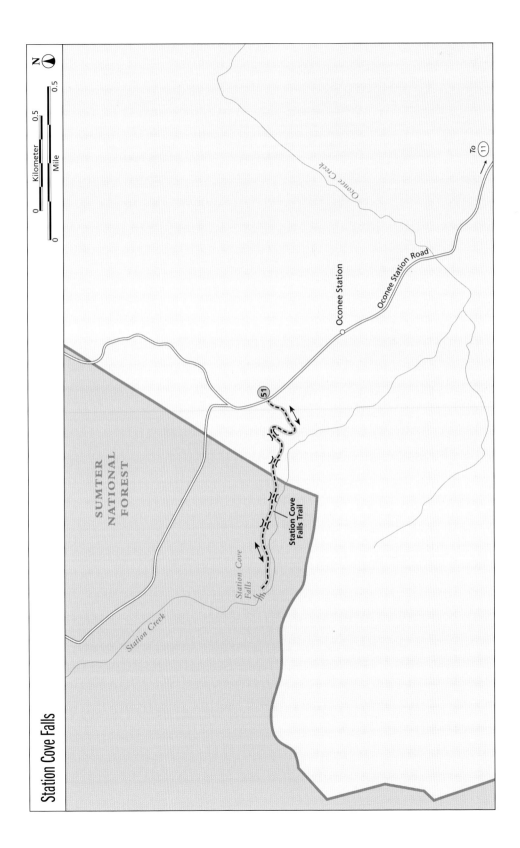

SUMTER
NATIONAL
FOREST

Station Creek

Station Cove
Falls

Station Cove
Falls Trail

Oconee Station

Oconee Station Road

Oconee Creek

To (11)

N

Kilometer
0   0.5

Mile
0   0.5

51

Station Cove Falls is, simply put, impressive.

structure in the South Carolina upcountry. This old stone building is the centerpiece of the park now, but in its day this was neither picnic nor park.

Originally built as a military compound to protect against the Creek and Cherokee tribes, ironically, it later became an Indian trading post and was used as such for many years.

Miles and Directions

0.0 From the trailhead, the wide trail heads west, straight back into the woods. Bypass any small side trails and stay on the main wide path.

0.3 Cross a wooden footbridge and continue hiking west-southwest.

0.4 Cross a second footbridge; continue to hike west.

0.5 Cross a third footbridge and continue hiking west.

0.6 Cross your final footbridge and immediately come to a fork at a fence. Go left and continue hiking west on the main trail.

0.7 The trail leads to the creek. Instead of crossing the creek, head right (northwest) and follow the creek upstream and slightly uphill.

0.8 Arrive at the base of Station Cove Falls (N34 50.965 / W83 05.117). Return the way you came.

1.6 Arrive back at the trailhead.

52 Twin Falls

Empowering! Twin Falls has so much to offer—from power and might to character and diversity—it easily lands on the Author's Favorites List. I highly recommend that you take the trip and embrace all the wonderful things this one has to offer.

Height: 100 feet	**County:** Pickens
Beauty rating: Excellent	**Land status:** Private nature preserve, Felburn
Distance: 0.6 mile out and back	Foundation
Difficulty: Easy	**Trail contact:** None
Trail surface: Wide, hard-packed dirt	**FYI:** Open dawn to dusk
Approximate hiking time: 20 minutes	**Maps:** *DeLorme: South Carolina Atlas & Gazet-*
Blaze color: No blazes	*teer:* Page 17 E6

Finding the trailhead: From the junction of US 178 and the North Carolina–South Carolina state line, drive south on US 178 for 7.4 miles. Turn right onto Cleo Chapman Highway (SC 100) and drive for 1.9 miles to a T intersection at Eastatoee Community Road. Turn right at the T and continue on Eastatoee Community Road for 0.9 mile. Turn right onto Water Falls Road, which soon becomes gravel. Follow the road as it winds around for 0.4 mile and dead-ends at a gate with a large fenced-off parking area to the left.

From the junction of US 178 and SC 11, drive north on US 178 for 3.0 miles. Turn left onto Cleo Chapman Highway (SC 100) immediately after passing Bob's Place and follow the directions above.

The trailhead is located at the northeast end of the parking area. GPS: N35 00.585 / W82 49.278

The Hike

Go around the gate and follow the wide, roadlike path as it heads northeast, straight back into the woods. As you make your way toward the falls, bypass any side trails that lead to the creek. Along the way, you pass a miniature waterwheel. From here the trail narrows and begins a slow ascent to the observation deck at the base of Twin Falls.

Located within the Felburn Foundation's nature preserve, Twin Falls has several aliases: Rock Falls, Reedy Cove Falls, and Eastatoe Falls, just to name a few.

Eastatoe is the Cherokee word for the Carolina parakeet (*Conuropsis carolinensis*). There was even an Eastatoe tribe known as the "Green Bird People." The parakeet, which once flourished in the Southeast, was the only parrot species native to mainland North America. Its range covered as far north as the Ohio Valley and extended south to the Gulf of Mexico. The bird has been extinct since 1918, when the last one, Incas, died in captivity at the Cincinnati Zoo.

Twin Falls

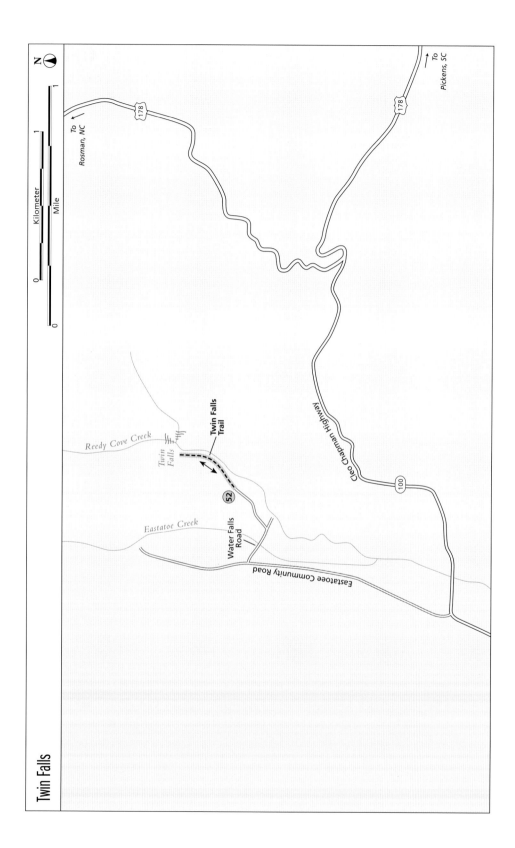

The Felburn Foundation and Hinkle family have done a wonderful job of preserving Reedy Cove.

Miles and Directions

0.0 From the trailhead, hike northeast on the wide trail as it heads straight back into the woods. Bypass any side trails to the creek and continue hiking northeast.

0.3 Arrive at an observation deck at the base of Twin Falls (N35 00.791 / W82 49.123). Return the way you came.

0.6 Arrive back at the trailhead.

53 Raven Cliff Falls

Intense! Raven Cliff Falls flows with power, grace, and great intensity. All 420 feet of it! This is certainly one of the tallest waterfalls in the East and the tallest in South Carolina.

Height: 420 feet
Beauty rating: Excellent
Distance: 4.4 miles out and back
Difficulty: Moderate
Trail surface: Wide gravel path and hard-packed dirt
Approximate hiking time: 2 hours, 30 minutes
Blaze color: Red
County: Greenville

Land status: State park
Trail contact: Caesars Head State Park; (864) 836-6115; www.southcarolinaparks.com
FYI: Small day-use fee per adult to hike; pay it at the ranger station or with exact change at a self-pay station at trailhead parking
Maps: *DeLorme: South Carolina Atlas & Gazetteer:* Page 17 D8; *DeLorme: North Carolina Atlas & Gazetteer:* Page 53 E6

Finding the trailhead: From the junction of US 276 and SC 11, drive north on US 276 for 8.6 miles to a parking area on the right at the sign for Raven Cliff Parking.

From the junction of US 276 and the North Carolina–South Carolina State Line, drive south on US 276 for 2.1 miles to a parking area on the left at the sign for Raven Cliff Parking. (If you miss the turn but see the Caesars Head State Park Office, which will be on the right as you're heading south, either ask inside or turn around and travel north for 1.0 mile to the parking area, which would now be on the right.)

The trailhead is located on the south side of US 276 (the opposite side from where you parked). GPS: N35 06.931 / W82 38.303

The Hike

The Raven Cliff Falls Trail takes you downhill on a wide gravel path and into the forest. At the bottom of the hill, go right at the fork and follow the red blazes. Cross a tiny creek, and the easily followed, well-maintained trail then meanders up and down through the forest. The trail leads down some steps and into the cool shade of rhododendron and mountain laurel.

Continue following the red blazes and come to a fork with the blue-blazed Gum Gap Trail to the right (northwest) and the red-blazed Raven Cliff Falls trail continuing left (south). Go left, making your way deeper into the Mountain Bridge Wilderness. When you come to another fork, with the Dismal Trail heading off to the left (south), keep right (southwest) following the wider Raven Cliff Falls Trail as it begins to climb. Follow it for another 0.1 mile to an observation deck with a distant view of Raven Cliff Falls from above.

▶ There are twenty-six named waterfalls within the Mountain Bridge Wilderness waiting to be explored. Detailed maps and information are available at the ranger station, located 1.0 mile south of the trailhead on US 276.

Raven Cliff Falls sits off in the distance amidst the Mountain Bridge Wilderness.

I recommend bringing binoculars or a good zoom lens to get the best views of this one, which sits far across the valley.

Raven Cliff Falls is located within Caesars Head State Park in the Mountain Bridge Wilderness Area. Although popular for the falls, the park is more specifically known, and named, for Caesars Head, a rocky outcrop that is said to resemble the head of Caesar. Part of the Bald Mountain pluton, this natural formation is estimated to be over 400 million years old.

Raven Cliff Falls

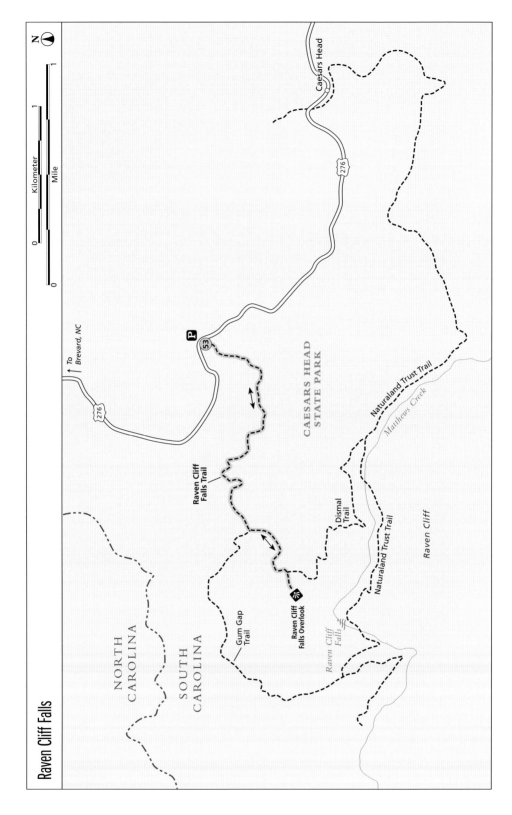

N

Kilometer

Mile

To Brevard, NC

276

P

53

276

Caesars Head

Raven Cliff Falls Trail

CAESARS HEAD STATE PARK

Gum Gap Trail

Dismal Trail

Naturaland Trust Trail

Naturaland Trust Trail

Matthews Creek

Raven Cliff Falls Overlook

Raven Cliff Falls

Raven Cliff

NORTH CAROLINA

SOUTH CAROLINA

This family has fun hiking across a suspension bridge.

Miles and Directions

0.0 From the trailhead, hike south as you follow the wide gravel path downhill.

0.3 Reach the bottom of the hill and go right (southwest) at the fork, following the red-blazed trail. Cross a tiny stream, and the trail meanders up and down through the forest.

0.9 Make your way down some steps and into the shade of rhododendron and mountain laurel. Continue hiking southwest, still following the red blazes.

1.6 Come to a fork with the blue-blazed Gum Gap Trail to the right (northwest). Go left here, staying with the red blazes on the Raven Cliff Falls Trail.

2.1 Come to another fork, with the Dismal Trail to your left (south) and the wider Raven Cliff Falls Trail to the right (southwest). Go right here, still following the Raven Cliff Falls Trail as it begins to climb.

2.2 Arrive at an observation deck for Raven Cliff Falls (N35 06.554 / W82 39.482). Return the way you came.

4.4 Arrive back at the trailhead.

Index

HELP US KEEP THIS GUIDE UP TO DATE

Every effort has been made by the author and editors to make this guide as accurate and useful as possible. However, many things can change after a guide is published—trails are rerouted, regulations change, techniques evolve, facilities come under new management, and so on.

We would appreciate hearing from you concerning your experiences with this guide and how you feel it could be improved and kept up to date. While we may not be able to respond to all comments and suggestions, we'll take them to heart, and we'll also make certain to share them with the author. Please send your comments and suggestions to the following address:

GPP
Reader Response/Editorial Department
P.O. Box 480
Guilford, CT 06437

Or you may e-mail us at: editorial@GlobePequot.com

Thanks for your input, and happy trails!

About the Author

Waterfall hunter, nature enthusiast, tree hugger, and avid hiker, Melissa Watson is truly at her best when she's in the forest. Her passion for waterfalls and nature in general stems back to childhood, and she continues to fulfill that passion to this day. For the past twenty years Melissa has been exploring the forests of Georgia and South Carolina—hiking by day and camping by night as she continues her quest for new trails and new waterfalls. And whether searching out new waterfalls or revisiting old favorites, she has come to be known as a local expert in the field.

Melissa is a career firefighter and paramedic, with eighteen years on the job. She has been adventure racing since 2000 and continues to master her skills as a navigator and mountaineer. She is also the author of the FalconGuide *Hiking Waterfalls in North Carolina*.

For more information on Melissa, visit her website at www.trailtimenow.com.

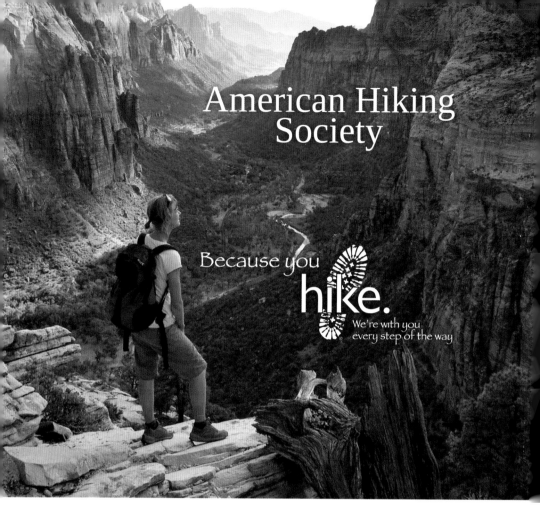

American Hiking Society

Because you **hike.**
We're with you every step of the way

As a national voice for hikers, **American Hiking Society** works every day:

- Building and maintaining hiking trails
- Educating and supporting hikers by providing information and resources
- Supporting hiking and trail organizations nationwide
- Speaking for hikers in the halls of Congress and with federal land managers

Whether you're a casual hiker or a seasoned backpacker, become a member of American Hiking Society and join the national hiking community! You'll enjoy great member benefits and help preserve the nation's hiking trails, so tomorrow's hike is even better than today's. We invite you to join us now!

American Hiking Society